John H. Pettingell

The Gospel of Life in the Syriac New Testament

John H. Pettingell

The Gospel of Life in the Syriac New Testament

ISBN/EAN: 9783337244927

Printed in Europe, USA, Canada, Australia, Japan

Cover: Foto ©Lupo / pixelio.de

More available books at **www.hansebooks.com**

THE GOSPEL OF LIFE

IN THE

SYRIAC NEW TESTAMENT.

THE SYRIAC, PESHITO, CONTRASTED WITH THE GREEK, WITH
RESPECT TO THE FOLLOWING WORDS, VIZ.:

(GREEK.)	(English Version of the Greek.)	(English Version of the Syriac.)
SŌZŌ.	**Save.**	To give **Life.**
SŌTĒRIA.	**Salvation.**	The gift of **Life.**
SŌTĒR.	**Savior.**	The **Life-Giver.**

BY J. H. PETTINGELL, A. M.

*Author of the "Homiletical Index," "Theological Trilemma,"
"Platonism versus Christianity," "Bible Terminology,"
"The Life Everlasting," "The Unspeakable Gift," "Lan-
guage—Its Nature and Functions," "The Two Ways,"
"Will Satan Live Forever?" "Human Immor-
tality," "Life and Death in the New Testa-
ment," "The Fact and Nature of the
Resurrection of the Dead," etc., etc.*

"Christ spoke and discoursed in the Syriac language." *Francius.*
"The greater part of the New Testament was *originally* written — I
believe — in Syriac, and not merely translated, in the Apostolic age."
Pres. E. Stiles, of Yale College.
"It is natural to suppose, from its great antiquity, that it must deviate in
many cases from the Greek manuscripts, the oldest of which were written
above four hundred years later, and are mostly the productions of countries remote from Syria." *Michaelis.*

YARMOUTH, ME.
SCRIPTURAL PUBLICATIO
ADDRESS, I. C. WELLC

Price, 15 Cents, by m

THE GOSPEL OF LIFE

—IN THE—

SYRIAC NEW TESTAMENT..

It is the opinion of many scholars, that the Hebrew was the original language of man; that it was given to our first parents directly from heaven; first, in the oral form, and afterward, in the time of Moses, and not till then, in written characters. For this opinion they urge many sound reasons. But, be this as it may, we know that the Hebrew language was the vernacular of the ancient Israelites, and that the Old Testament Scriptures, some parts in prose and some in poetry, excepting a few fragmentary parts, were written in Hebrew.

The language of the Chaldeans, by whom the Jews were carried into captivity, about 600 years before Christ, was a branch of the same root, though it differed widely in both its oral and written form. In consequence of their long detention in the country of the Chaldeans, the pure Hebrew tongue of the Jews became corrupted, and after their return to Syria, it was still further corrupted by their subjugation to other nations, and by the importation of other races into their country: so that, at the commencement of the Christian era, their vernacular,—though still retaining the general characteristics of the old Hebrew,—had become what is called the Syro-Chaldaic, or Syriac language. This was divided into two principal dialects; the Eastern Aramean, which prevailed along the Southern and Eastern coasts of Syria; and the Western Aramean, which prevailed in the regions to the North and West. These dialects, however, were substantially the same language, differing more in the form of the written characters employed and in the pronunciation of the words, than in the words themselves.

After the conquest of this country by Alexander, in the fourth century before Christ, the Greek language was introduced, and came generally to prevail as the language of the learned and ruling classes, throughout Syria and all the surrounding regions. Still later, in the century before Christ, the Latin tongue was introduced by their Roman conquerors. Though it had some standing, as the language of their rulers and law-givers, it was never very extensively used in this part of Asia; but, after a time, it came to prevail to a considerable extent, to the West of Syria, and especially in Europe, as the language of the educated classes.

Thus, it will be seen that, at the beginning of the Christian era, there were three languages, — not to notice others of minor importance,— that prevailed to a greater or less extent, in Syria or Palestine: The Syriac or Syro-Chaldaic, which was the vernacular of the common people, of the synagogues and other public assemblies of the Jews; The Greek, which was the language of what are commonly called the upper classes, the educated and the refined; The Latin, which was the language of the government to which they were subject.

The state of things, with respect to diversity of tongues, in Palestine, in the time of Christ, was similar to that which now obtains in some of our larger cities, and especially, some of the cities and countries of the Old World. Take, for example, the city of Antwerp, in Belgium, with which, — having resided there for several years, — I am familiar. The basilar language of the people is Flemish, which is a corrupt form of the Dutch. Every citizen is supposed to be able to understand, and to use this language, both in its spoken and written form. The uneducated and laboring classes know no other. It is the vernacular of the streets, of the workshops, of the markets, and of most of the Churches. But the French also prevails very extensively. It is the language of business and trade among all the higher classes. It is taught in their schools, and is the ruling language of their higher seminaries of learning, of their literary, artistic, and social circles. No one makes any pretension to a fair education, who has not added to his native Flemish, a knowledge of the French also. The streets of the city have two names; one in Flemish, and the other in French. The daily papers, in each of these languages, circulate side by side, and men of affairs take and read both. Beside these, both the English and the German are used to a considerable extent, especially by the merchants. It is not difficult for an Englishman or an American, who is familiar with only his own tongue, to do business in most of the principal shops, and to make himself understood at the hotels of the city.

That our Lord, whose intercourse was chiefly with the common people, preached and taught in their own Syriac vernacular, there is no doubt. "The common people heard Him gladly." Indeed it is not certain that He ever used any other. He grew up among them as a laborer, and probably had no other education as a child, or mere man, than was common with the class to which He belonged. Of course, I am not speaking of His knowledge as a divine person. The same is true of His twelve Apostles, and His more immediate disciples. That all of them were familiar with the spoken Syriac, there is no question. How many of them were sufficiently educated to be able to read or write it, or whether any of them were familiar with the Greek, which would indicate a still higher education, and if so, which of them, must be a matter of conjecture. We know that most of them were taken from the lower walks of life, and those of them who were natives of Galilee, no doubt, spoke with the brogue, which was common in that region, and which differed from that of Judea, as perhaps that of Scotland differs from that of England. When Peter denied his Lord in Jerusalem, his speech betrayed his Galilean origin.

The inscription over the cross, THE KING OF THE JEWS, was written in the three prevailing languages; Hebrew (or Syriac), Greek, and Latin, that it might be read by all classes. Here, perhaps, we may see an unwitting prophecy of His future universal Kingship. When the chief priests would have had it changed to "He said, I am King of the Jews," Pilate showed a little of the firmness he so sadly lacked in giving Him over to their will, by replying, "What I have written, I have written."

That Paul, as an educated man, the divinely commissioned Apostle to the Gentiles, was familiar with both the Hebrew-Syriac and Greek languages, and perhaps also,— aside from his supernatural endowments,— with the Latin, and other languages is quite probable. But he expressly tells us that, when the Lord revealed Himself to him, on the way to Damascus, He spoke to him in the Hebrew (that is, in the Syro-Chaldaic) tongue. No doubt, also, Paul's missionary companions, such as Silas, Barnabas, Mark, Luke, and Timothy,— none of whom, however, were of the twelve Apostles,— were well educated for their work. When Paul had been rescued from the violence of the mob at Jerusalem, Claudius Lysias, the chief captain, who had rescued him, not knowing his antecedents, seems to have been suprised that he could speak Greek, and was glad to confer, privately, with him in that tongue. Then, when he had permitted him to address the surging multitude, that were thirsting for his blood, Paul beckoned with his hand, and began to address them in their own vernacular; and when they heard that he spoke in the Hebrew tongue, they kept the more silence.

The foregoing remarks are introductory to the more interesting and important inquiry: *In what language, or languages, were the twenty-seven books of the New Testament first written?* It may not be so easy as many seem to suppose, to answer this question, which has taxed the scholarship of our most learned biblical scholars for many generations, in a perfectly satisfactory manner, with respect to some of these books, nor, indeed, with respect to any of them; for none of the original manuscripts are known to exist. Although there are many old manuscripts now extant, in Greek,

Syriac, Coptic, Latin, Gothic, and other tongues, containing parts, or in some cases, nearly, if not quite the whole of our present canon, there are none that reach back beyond the fourth century of the Christian era; and these, of course, must be translations, or copies of still older ones, now lost. These manuscripts vary, to a greater or less degree, from each other. There are said to have been found not less than one hundred thousand variations in such of the Greek manuscripts alone, as have been collated,—most of them, minute and of little apparent importance, but still, they show how impossible it is to be sure of the exact words, or ideas of the original; even supposing that to have been the Greek, which can only be a matter of inference, at the best. The only way of deciding what is the true reading of any passage in which these manuscripts differ, as well as what was the language in which the first manuscripts were written, from which these later ones have been copied, or translated, is by a careful comparison of all these various codices with each other, and by the citations that are found in the writings of the Fathers, and by such hints or more positive statements as may be found in them; and then it becomes simply a question of the weight of evidence bearing on one side or the other. There is hardly any question of importance, with regard to the authorship of any one of those books, or the original language in which it was written, or to any important diversity of reading, that has not given rise to conflicting views, or opinions, among learned men, which they have stoutly contested. It is only by a majority, or two-thirds vote, according to previous agreement, that our translators, or revisers, have been able to determine these questions among themselves.

The amount of learning and research that has been expended on these questions, during the centuries, is immense. No one man, however diligent he might be, could possibly possess himself of all that has been written on them, were he to devote a long life to this special study. All that any ordinary student of the

Scripture — without professing to be an adept in Oriental literature and paleontological science, — can hope to do, is to make himself acquainted, as far as he is able, with the gist of what these scholars have written, and then, with their help, and by his own independent study, to satisfy himself as best he can in regard to these matters.

I propose nothing more in this paper than, in a modest way, to give the results of my own inquiry in this line, for the consideration of others.

1. The common impression that the entire New Testament was first written in Greek, and that all the copies we now have, in whatever tongue, are copies, or translations of the original manuscripts, when seriously examined, is found to have no certain foundation. And yet this has been taken almost universally, for granted. It is probable, that this is true with respect to some, possibly a majority of these books. But it is more than probable, if not quite certain, that some portions of the New Testament, such as the Gospel of Matthew, the Epistles to the Hebrews, and others, which will hereafter be mentioned, were first written in the vernacular Syriac of the Jews, and were afterward translated into Greek; and that other portions, perhaps most of the books, were duplicated, at the time they were written, by their authors, or under their direction, — one copy being furnished to those who were familiar with the Greek, and another to those who knew only the Syriac.

2. The reason why such a strong partiality has been shown to the Greek, over all others, by the translators and revisers of our English versions, and the true reading of disputed passages has been determined almost wholly by the most reliable of the Greek manuscripts, is easily accounted for, when we consider the commanding position which was held by the language and the philosophy of the Greeks, in the early ages of the Church. The almost universal prevalence of this language — supplemented by the Latin, which afterward came into vogue — as the classical language of religion, of literature and of science, the knowledge

1*

of which was indispensable to a liberal education, has tended to this result.

The Christian Church came early, after the days of the Apostles, under the influence, not merely of the Greek language, but of the philosophy of the Greeks. The tendency in this direction was apparent even in the times of the Apostles. It was against this very influence that Paul so often, and earnestly warned the early Christians; "Beware lest any man spoil you through philosophy and vain deceit, after the tradition of men, after the rudiments of the world, and not after Christ." "Avoid profane and vain babblings, and oppositions of science, falsely so-called, which some professing, have erred concerning the faith." "I fear lest by any means, as the serpent beguiled Eve through his subtilty, so your minds should be corrupted from the simplicity that is in Christ." Almost immediately after the Pentecostal ingathering into the Church, we find a murmuring among the Grecians against the Hebrews, "because their widows were neglected in the daily ministrations." In order to satisfy them, and to make sure that they were properly cared for, seven men, all of whom bear Grecian names, were chosen deacons. Though Stephen, one of them, contended so boldly with "the Libertines, and Cyrenians, and Alexandrians, and them of Asia and Cilicia, that they were not able to resist the wisdom and spirit by which he spoke," yet we find them coming more and more under the influence of these and other worldly factions, and it was not long before the Grecian philosophy had become dominant and controlling. Their schools of literature, and especially of theology, were Grecian schools. Grecian philosophers became their teachers and leaders. This was the language they used in their lectures, and other discourses. Meanwhile the vernacular of the Jewish converts, even in Syria, fell more and more into desuetude, and at length became so nearly obsolete as a spoken language, that their Syriac Scriptures, that continued to be read in their Churches, needed some one to interpret them to the people. For it is a matter of history, that they had the Scripture canon, in this language, even before the close of the First Century; and they have always clung to it with great tenacity, down to modern times.

The first one or two generations after the time of Christ are almost barren of any Christian literature that is now extant: but after this, came Justin, Theophilus, Irenæus, Athenagoras, Origen, and others, whose Greek manuscripts, that have been preserved, contain numerous Scripture citations. Greek copies of the Scriptures, in whole or in part, were greatly multiplied during these early and subsequent ages of the Church, before the invention of printing, so that there are said to be known to European scholars, some sixteen hundred, or more of them, now in existence. It is also said that citations from these early copies are so abundant, in the writings of the Fathers, that, if all of the originals were to be destroyed, it would be possible to restore the whole of the New Testament from their writings. Latin versions from the Greek were also very early made, as early probably, as the beginning of the Second Century, and many of them, though very imperfect, became quite numerous, especially in the Western Churches.

When we take into account the fact that versions of the Scripture in languages, other than the Greek and and Latin, were comparatively rare, and but little known in Europe, and the languages in which they were written were not generally cultivated by biblical scholars, it is not difficult to understand why the Latin and the Greek, especially the latter, have had such a paramount influence in determining the rendering of our English version. "It is admitted by critics that the learned men of Europe were ignorant of the very existence of a New Testament in Syriac, until 1552, when they heard of it at Rome, from Moses of Mardin. They then took steps to get an edition of it, and the cost was borne by the Emperor of Germany, Ferdinand I. But for nearly fifteen centuries, the Syrian Christians had firmly adhered to it as a truly apostolic document. It is true, more than one attempt was made to break through their attachment to it, and win them over to a Greek representation of apostolic teaching, but it could not succeed. They knew their ground too well to suffer either Philocenias, in the sixth century, or Thomas of Heraclea, with his bundle of Greek manuscripts gathered at Alexandria in Egypt, in 616, to win them over to another Testament. The adhesion of the Syrian Churches from the beginning, for eighteen centuries till now, has been as constant and as cordial, as ever happened to any New Testament in the World. But this statement is far too feeble, for to no other version, or text, has there been any such unswerving adhesion." *

When Dr. James Murdock undertook the translation of the Syriac (Peshito) New Testament into English, in 1845, he supposed, as he tells us, that he was producing the first translation of these Syriac Scriptures into English, that had ever been made. It was not until he had completed it, that he learned that an English gentleman, Mr. J. W. Etheridge, was engaged in the same task.†

But now as the Peshito is becoming better known, and its great antiquity — even if it does not ante-date all other texts — is universally admitted, its value as an auxiliary to the interpretation of Scripture, is conceded by all competent scholars.

3. It would seem to have a claim to equal, if not paramount authority, in determining the reading of disputed passages. For it is to be remembered, that the Syriac was the vernacular of the Jews, in the time of our Lord, and the very language which He used in addressing them, as well as the language of

---

* Mr. James Holding, an English scholar, from one of whose articles, in the *Rainbow*, London, the above paragraph is cited, has given me some valuable suggestions in these articles on this question. I have followed him in the English orthography of certain Syriac words.

† There are three different Syriac versions of the New Testament: The *Peshito*, The *Philoxenian*, and The *Hierosolymitan*. Dr. Murdock's English version is made from the first, which is not only the oldest, but altogether the most reliable. The term *Peshito* means clear, explicit, easy to be understood. I take this occasion to acknowledge my great indebtedness to this version. It has been constantly before me in preparing this paper, though I have not always adopted his verbal renderings.

His Apostles in addressing the people of Palestine. In the record which was made of the words of Christ by the Evangelists in the four Gospels, they would naturally, if not necessarily, first write them out in the very language He employed. Even if it could be shown that any of them wrote their narrative in Greek, they would, even in this case, be under the necessity of translating His words from the Syriac in which He spoke, into the Greek, and then, instead of the original, we should have but a translation at best. But it is by no means to be taken for granted that these sacred writers gave such signal and exclusive preference to the Greek, over their own tongue, as is generally supposed.

The question as to each of these books cannot here be considered in detail; but it may be summarily said that, it is generally conceded that MATTHEW wrote his Gospel in Syriac; for it was written expressly for the Hebrews. This is the opinion of Papias, Eusebius, Epiphaneus, Jerome, and of other Fathers, as well as of not a few modern scholars, and even those who give their preference to the Greek, admit that a Syriac copy might have been prepared at the same time. It is the opinion of Olshausen, that Matthew prepared two copies, either by his own hands, or by the assistance of others, one in Syriac for the Hebrews, and the other in Greek for those who required it.

As for MARK and LUKE, neither of whom were of the twelve Apostles, but as the associates of Paul, were probably familiar with the Greek tongue, and who wrote more especially for the Gentiles, it is not unreasonable to suppose that they would furnish transcripts for the Syrian Christians in their own tongue. Eusebius supposes, that Mark, whom tradition credits with having been Peter's companion and interpreter, wrote his Gospel from the dictation of that Apostle.

I have never seen any good reason for supposing, with some, that JOHN wrote his Gospel in his extreme old age, sixty or seventy years after the death of Christ. He records more of our Lord's words than all the other Evangelists together. It is not possible, without a miracle, that he should have remembered them so long, and been able to record them so minutely, nor is it reasonable to suppose, that he would have deferred this duty to so late a period. I am inclined to believe, with Drs. Lardner, Owen, Michaelis, and others, that it was written about the year 65: and with Salmatius, Grotius, Bolton, and others, that he first composed it in Syriac, for it is only in this language he could give the very words of our Lord Himself. There is no objection to believing, however, that at the same time, or soon afterward, another copy was prepared in Greek.

We notice in the Greek manuscripts of all the Gospels, but more especially in that of Mark, the occurrence of Syriac idioms, and words, with an explanation introduced, by way of parenthesis, which would be quite natural in translating from this language to another, in the case of words and phrases that could not well be exactly rendered, or that were more emphatic in the original. Thus, we are told, in our Greek versions, that Christ said to the maid, when He restored her to life, *Talitha-cumi*, and then, in parenthesis, in the Greek version we are informed that this means *Damsel arise:* but no such explanation is given in the Syriac, or original, for the very good reason that it is not needed, for it is all in the same language: and so when He said *Ephatha*, to the deaf man, we are told in the Greek, that it means *Be opened:* and so of *Abba*, that it means *Father*, and of *Corban*, that it means *Gift*, of *Raca*, that it means *Fool*, and *Golgotha*, a *skull*, etc. These are all Hebrew-Syriac words, which appear to have been transferred unchanged from the original manuscript, into the Greek, with a parenthetical explanation. Both Matthew and Mark record the dying words of our Lord, just as He uttered them; *Eloi, Eloi, lama sabacthani*, and then, in the Greek copy or version of Mark's Gospel, we are informed, in Greek, that these words mean, *My God, My God, why hast thou forsaken me?*

There is no question, but that scattered manuscripts of the several books of the New Testament, in Greek,

were in existence very early, for the Fathers quote
from them,—but there is no evidence that any attempt was made to collect them into one code, or
canon, till after the Second or Third Century. But it
is certain, on the other hand, that the Syrian Churches
had their canon long before this collection was made;
tradition says, between the years 55 and 60, and that
this was done by the Apostle Jude. This canon is
known to have contained all the books now included
in our New Testament, excepting the Apocalypse,
and the brief Epistles of 2d Peter, 2d and 3d John,
and Jude. This tradition is strongly corroborated
by the fact, that these closing portions of our present
canon were not then written; and this is a good
and sufficient reason why they were not included in
the first collection. The abrupt closing of the Book of
Acts—for it was evidently written at about that time
—that it might be ready for inclusion in this collection, goes to confirm the tradition as to the date of
this collection. The Apocalypse and the four short
Epistles which were not in readiness to be included at
that early date, were afterward received into the
Syriac Canon, but not till the sixth century.

By whom this first collection of Syriac manuscripts
was made, must be a matter of conjecture and inference. It has been supposed by some writers, and not
without reason, that the editing was done by the
Apostle Jude, and that he was assisted in the labor of
collecting them from their various sources by Silas,
the companion of Paul, and that we are indebted to
him, and not to Paul, for the Epistle to the Hebrews.
That this Epistle was written first in the vernacular
of the Syrian Christians is very generally conceded.
It is not improbable that Paul, though he might have
written most, or all of his Epistles in Greek,—which
he was well able to do,—would have taken care that the
Syrian Christians and others, who spoke the Syriac
language, should be furnished with copies which they
could read. For while Paul and the other writers
addressed their manuscripts to particular Churches or
classes of persons, writing under inspiration, they evi-

dently wrote for the Church at large, not only in their own day, but for all coming time; and if their writings were needed in more than one tongue to make them more generally useful, it is not unreasonable to believe that they would take some pains to provide for this want. Indeed, we see that Paul, in writing to the Colossians gives special directions, that his Epistle be read also in the Church at Laodicea, and vice versa.

That my own conclusions as to the importance and authoritative character of the Syriac New Testament may not seem to be peculiar to myself, and without good reason, let me refer to what some others, who have made this subject a special study, and whose opinions are not to be despised, have said in regard to it:

"It may be noticed that we write Syriac *readings*, and not *renderings*, and this we do advisedly, for we wish to avoid words which would lead the reader to think that we admit that his Syriac is only a version from Greek. We see proof ever augmenting that the Peshito is no translation, but an original production of the first writers, slightly revised, perhaps, and enriched, by here and there, a note from the pen of inspired revisers, but in its main bulk, the work of those holy men whom Jesus told the Jews, in His last public discourse, would yet appear and make a final appeal to the nation before its final overthrow. These were His words: "Behold I send you prophets, wise men and writers." This last part of His intended gifts is obscured to our people, when translators retain the word "Scribes," and this antiquated Latinism is retained in the revised New Testament. The Saxon word, *Writers*, is better known, and of more modern use. Is there not a little pedantry, in our learned revisers reproducing the half-antiquated word, *Scribes?* It was not such a class of men as the Jewish Scribes that Jesus meant to send, but men who could write His memoirs, and direct the faith and practice of His people." *James Holding.*

"The Peshito is the very best translation of the Greek Testament that I have ever read. The affinity of the Syriac to the dialect of Palestine is so great as to justify, in some respects, the assertion that the Syriac translator has recorded the actions and speeches of Christ, in the very language in which He spoke. The difference between the dialect which was spoken by Christ, and that of the Syriac translator, consisted almost wholly in the mode of pronouncing. It is natural to suppose, from its great antiquity, that it must deviate in many cases from the Greek manuscripts, the oldest of which were written above four hundred years later, and are mostly the productions of countries remote from Syria." *Michaelis.*

"Let those who speak lightly of this version, know that the Syriac, if not the very language in which Christ Himself conversed with His Apostles, approaches very nearly to the vernacular tongue of our Savior, and His companions, and that into it the recent books of the New Testament were the first of all translated, and that, too, at the very time when the Apostles were laying the first foundation of the Christian Church among the nations. I admit that it is a version, but it is the first and most ancient of all versions. It is to be preferred before all others, as being more authentic and more correct. Made either by some one of the Evangelists, or certainly by one of those who had the Apostles present with them at Antioch, whom they could consult, and hear speak on many of the obscure passages. And therefore to this version only can we safely go, when any obscurity or difficulty occurs in the original Greek. This only can be safely consulted, and relied upon, whenever there is doubt respecting the import or rendering of any passage." *Professor Martini.*

"This version, all the learned pronounce, and declare to be the purest of all versions, and doubtless it was so exactly transferred by holy men, because Christ spoke and discoursed in the Syriac language; so that we cannot doubt, that the Apostles and apostolical men carefully inquired after and laid up the very words of Christ, and with holy veneration endeavored to record them in their version. . . . Among all the versions of the New Testament, that which holds the first rank, and is the most exact, felicitous and divine, is certainly the Syriac, which, undoubtedly, was most faithfully handed down by apostolical men, who remembered well the recently uttered words of Christ and His Apostles, and understood their meaning. For Christ Himself used this language." *Professor Francius.*

"It is entirely consonant with truth, that this version was formed at the very commencement of the Christian Church, either by the Apostles themselves, or by their disciples; unless we should suppose, that, in writing they had regard only to strangers, and cared little or nothing for their own countrymen." *Emanuel Tremelius.*

"From these most ancient versions we infer that this language is of the highest importance, because the writers of the New Testament to whom this language was vernacular, first preached the Divine Oracles in it to the Jews and the nations around them, and *afterward wrote them out in Greek,* yet retaining the spirit of the Syriac. Nay, it was the vernacular of the Lord and Savior Himself. He drew it in with His mother's milk, and in it the Only-begotten Son of God revealed to the world the will of God and the express promise of *Eternal Life.* This language He consecrated by

His holy lips; in this language He taught the doctrines of the Gospel; in it He offered His prayers to the Father, laid open the mysteries hidden from the world, and heard the voice of the Father coming from heaven; so that we may say, *Lingua hominum est lingua nobilitata Dei."* *Bryan Walton.*

Dr. Murdock, who cites some of the above-mentioned authors and others, says: "The great value of this translation depends on its high antiquity, on the competence and fidelity of the translators, and on the near affinity of its language to that spoken by our Lord and His Apostles. In all these respects it stands pre-eminent among the numerous versions of the New Testament." Prof. Bolton, in his German translation of the Epistles, maintains that *nearly all the Epistles must have been first composed by the Apostles in Aramean, their native tongue,* and then committed by them to some of their Gerecizing companions, by whom they were translated into Greek before their publication. Bertholdt expresses the same opinion. He thinks that, after due time for reflection, the learned world will generally come to it, for such a hypothesis does not militate against the authority of the Greek, because it supposes the Greek translation to have been made by the special direction of the Apostles, and to have been inspected and fully approved by them. But it does show us that the Syriac version may be something more than a mere translation, and may have nearly or quite equal authority with Greek.

Dr. Ezra Stiles, late President of Yale College, in his Inaugural Address, says: "Kindred with this [the Hebrew] is the *Syriac, in which the greater part of the New Testament,* I believe, *was originally written,* and not merely translated, in the Apostolic age. The Syriac New Testament, therefore, is of high authority; nay, with me, of the same authority as the Greek." As for myself, without making any pretension of unusual scholarship, I cannot but concur in the opinion of these two last cited authorities.

4. Though there is found to be a substantial agreement between the Syriac and the Greek Scriptures, on

all the fundamental doctrines of the Gospel; and
though their differences are mainly with respect to the
integrity of certain passages that are included in the
one and not in the other, and as to the rendering of
others that are found in both, yet no critical reader
can fail to notice the greater prominence that is given
to the central Gospel doctrine of LIFE, — ETERNAL
LIFE ONLY IN CHRIST, in the Syriac Scriptures, and
how much more emphatically, He is here set forth as
— not merely the Savior, but as — the LIFE-GIVER of
men.

It is true this great truth stands out very prominently in all our versions — it could not be otherwise
in any fair version — but still, there is often an ambiguity or vagueness of enunciation in the Greek, that is
not found in the Syriac, and this is still greater in our
English version that is made from the Greek. In the
Greek, there are two words *psuchē* and *zōē* that stand
for " life "; the former refers exclusively to our natural, temporal life, and as such, is contrasted with natural death; the latter is always employed when the
higher life of the world beyond, which we receive
only by a new birth, is in question, and to this the
epithet *aiōnios*, signifying eternal, is commonly
joined; and to render it still more emphatic, the definite article (*hē*) "the" is prefixed; as *hē zōē aiōnios*
" The Life Everlasting"; and this higher life is contrasted with the death that is final and remediless,
otherwise called, "The Second Death." Now this
word *psuchē* occurs more than one hundred times in
the Greek New Testament, and always, invariably,
refers to a life that is transitory in man or animals;
and the word *zōē*, either with or without the adjective
signifying eternal, occurs, at least one hundred and
fifty times, and is always employed when the divine,
higher life is spoken of, and scarcely in any other
sense. It seems to have been set apart and consecrated to this special end in the Scriptures, of setting
forth the peculiar life of the children of God by a new
birth. But unfortunately, we have but the one word
life, — unless the word soul, which is quite ambiguous,

be used, — in our English version by which to designate these two sorts of life, and consequently, the
English reader often fails to observe the broad, and
indeed, the infinite distinction there actually is
between them. The Greek, therefore, in the clearness
with which this distinction is indicated, is much superior to our English version. But the Syriac is much
superior to both, in its treatment of the words *Save*,
Savior, *Salvation*, bearing on the same general question. For Salvation may have respect either to this
life, or the life to come; for example: When the disciples, in the tempest on the sea of Galilee, came to
Jesus in their distress saying, "Lord save us; we
perish," or when Peter, who was trying to walk on the
same sea, on another occasion, cried out, "Lord, save
me," the salvation in question was evidently a temporal salvation, a rescue from bodily peril; and Christ
may be called their Savior without any regard to His
higher prerogative, as the Savior of sinners. But
when the Samaritans said of Him, at the well of
Sychar, " This is indeed the Christ, the Savior of the
world," or when one asked Him, " Lord, are there few
that be saved?" that higher salvation, which it is the
express object of the Gospel to announce through
Christ, is evidently meant.

Here then, there are two sorts of salvation, a lower
and physical, and a higher and spiritual salvation
spoken of in the Scriptures. In the Syriac they are
always distinguished by separate words; but in the
Greek, and in our version, which follows the Greek,
they are both included under one broad term. Thus
we have *sōzō*, to save; *Sōtēr*, Savior; *Sōtēria*, salvation. But in the Syriac, the higher act of saving to
eternal life, the agent by which it is effected, and the
great salvation itself, are all designated by the use of
the root word *Khya* denoting Life-giving, the Life-
Giver, the gift of Life, and when a mere rescue or
deliverance of any sort is spoken of, another word is
employed, as *parak*, *parakna*, or some other word to
express it.

As our version is made from the Greek, the same

ambiguity in the use of the words "to Save," "Savior,"
"Salvation," runs through our English Scriptures.
Indeed, the ambiguity is still greater, for while two
separate words in the Greek are employed to distin-
guish between our physical life and the new life of
the world to come; viz.: *psuchē* and *zōē*, we have in
English, as we have seen, but the one word "*life*," to
express them both. But as I have remarked at length
on this point elsewhere,* I pass on to the more special
object of this paper: The treatment of the words
"Save," "Savior," "Salvation," in the Syriac, compared with what is found in the Greek and English
versions. This is a point to which sufficient attention
has not been given, by those who have discussed this
question of *Immortality or Eternal Life only in
Christ.*

5. It is agreed on all hands that we are saved by
Christ, that He is a great Savior, and this salvation
is a great salvation. But when we come to consider
the nature of this salvation, we differ widely from our
opponents. They assert that it is not from actual
death and destruction to a new life that is everlasting;
for all men are by nature possessed of a life that is
everlasting. It is therefore from sin and misery everlasting, that men are saved. But when we turn to the
Syriac Scriptures, which record the very words of our
Lord and of His immediate followers, we find this
salvation spoken of not as a mere rescue, or deliverance FROM evil, but also as the impartation of a LIFE.
Christ is set forth not simply as a Savior; He is all
this, but He is infinitely more, He is a LIFE-GIVER.
And when sinners are saved, they are not simply rescued from sin and misery or from death, but a new
life, a divine life, the life of the Savior which is immortal, is imparted to them. If then, due credit be
given to the Syriac Scriptures, our opponents can no
longer find shelter under those ambiguous terms, in
the Greek and English versions, nor evade the issue to
which we would hold them; that the Salvation of the

* See The Life Everlasting: The Unspeakable Gift; Life and Death in the
New Testament, etc.

Gospel is not a mere rescue, recovery or deliverance ; it is all this, but infinitely more, it is pre-eminently THE GIFT OF ETERNAL LIFE THROUGH JESUS CHRIST OUR LORD, THE ONLY LIFE-GIVER OF PERISHING MEN.

I have gone carefully through the Greek New Testament, and noted every instance of the occurrence of either of the words *Sōzō, Sōtēr,* or *Sōtēria,* and compared each passage with the parallel passage in the Syriac Peshito, and will now submit the result of this examination to the consideration of those who are interested in this inquiry. I find that the verb *sōzō,* to save, under its various inflections occurs eighty-seven times; the noun *Sōtēr,* Savior, eighteen times ; the noun *Sōtēria* or *Soterion,* Salvation, thirty-seven times. It will be hardly necessary to cite every case, where the same thought and form of expression are repeated. But I will cite the great majority of the cases — indeed, all that involve anything new, or that call for any special notice.

I. MATTHEW.

SYRIAC.

1: 21 Thou shalt call His name Jesus, for He will (*sō-sei*) *save* His people from their sins.

He will cause to LIVE again (or resuscitate) His people from their sins.

That is to say, He will give them life again from the death, which is the penalty of sin. This agrees with the words " The wages of sin is death ; but the gift of God is Eternal Life through Jesus Christ our Lord."

8: 25 And the disciples came to Him and awoke Him saying: "Lord (*sōson*) *save* us, we perish."

Saying " Our Lord (*patsyn*) *deliver* us; we are perishing."

In this case, it was merely temporal rescue or deliverance, they asked, and so it is the lower word (*patsah*) that is employed.

9: 21 For she said within herself, If I may but touch His garment, I shall be (*sōthēsomai*) *whole*.

22 But Jesus turned Him about, and when He saw her, He said, Daughter, be of good comfort; thy faith hath made thee (*sesōke*) *whole*. And the woman was made (*esōthē*) *whole* from that hour.

She had said in her mind, "If I but touch His garment I shall be *cured*." And Jesus turned Him and looked at her, and said: Take courage my daughter, thy faith hath given thee LIFE, and the woman was *cured* from that very hour.

Here, while in the Greek the word *sōzō* is used three times; the first and the last times referring to a bodily cure or deliverance, and the second only to the higher gift that was bestowed in answer to faith; we have in the Syriac two words to indicate this difference, and the higher word denoting the *Life* of the world to come, is employed only in the second instance.

10: 22 And ye shall be hated of all men for my name's sake: but he that endureth to the end shall be (*sōthēsetai*) *saved*.

He that shall endure to the end shall have LIFE.

There is no temporal deliverance promised to the persecuted in this passage; the promise has evident reference to the Eternal Life of the world to come. This is made apparent in the Syriac, but not in the Greek.

14: 30 But when he saw the wind boisterous, he was afraid; and beginning to sink, he cried, saying, Lord, (*sōson*) *save* me.

And he raised his voice and said: "Lord, *rescue* me."

It was evidently a bodily or temporal rescue that Peter asked for in this case, and this is all that is indicated in the Syriac.

18: 11 For the Son of man is come to (*sōsai*) *save* that which was lost.

For the Son of man hath come to give LIFE to that which was lost.

Here again, it appears in the Syriac, but not in the Greek, that the object of Christ in coming to the world was, not simply to save or rescue men from evil, but to bestow the boon of *Life* upon those who had forfeited everything by sin.

19: 25 When His disciples heard it, they were exceedingly amazed, saying, Who then can *be (sōthēnai) saved?*

Who then can attain to *(khya)* LIFE ?

This is the exclamation of the disciples after hearing what Christ said to the young man, who came to inquire " What good thing shall I do that I may have *(zōēn aiōnion)* eternal life ? " and when the young man had gone away sorrowful, He took occasion to tell them how difficult it is for a rich man to enter into the kingdom of heaven. This calls forth their exclamation of surprise, as above. It is evident that they understood by having eternal life and entering into the kingdom of heaven, the same thing. This is made to appear by the use of the higher word in the Syriac, but in the Greek it is vaguely called being saved.

24: 13 But he that shall endure unto the end, the same shall be *(sōthēsetai) saved.*

He that shall persevere to the end shall have LIFE.

Here again, the true nature of this salvation is declared only in the Syriac. It is not a mere rescue or salvation *from* sin and consequent misery, but it is the bestowment of an actual gift — the gift of *Life* that is promised.

27: 40 Thou that destroyest the temple, and buildest it in three days, *(sōson) save* thyself. If thou be the Son of God, come down from the cross.

Destroyer of the temple and Builder of it in three days; *deliver* thyself, if thou art the Son of God and come down from the cross.

42 He *(esōzen) saved* others; Himself He cannot *(sōsai) save.*

He gave LIFE to others [or rather professed to do it], His own life He cannot *save.*

49 The rest said, Let be, let us see whether Elias will come to *(sōzōn) save* Him.

Desist: we will see if Elijah will come to *rescue* Him.

Here we have the Greek verb *sōzō* four times repeated by those who mocked Christ on the cross. In the first and last cases, they are speaking only of a rescue or deliverance from the cruel death they are inflicting upon Him ; in the other two cases, they are taunting Him with the doctrine He had preached con-

cerning the life of the world to come, and concerning
Himself as the Giver of that life. These two ideas
are not distinguished in the Greek, but in the Syriac,
they are kept distinct by the use of two separate
words. For in the first and last cases, a word signifying *rescue* is used, but in the other two cases the word
signifying the impartation of LIFE is employed.

II. MARK.

It will not be important to *re*-cite under this Gospel
the cases occurring in the parallel passages in Matthew, unless some peculiarity attaches to them.

	SYRIAC.
5: 23 My little daughter lieth at the point of death: I pray thee, come and lay thy hands on her that she may be (*sōthē*) *healed;* and she shall live.	Come and lay thy hand on her and she will be *cured* and will live.

The ruler of the synagogue desired simply the
restoration of his daughter to health, her rescue from
the fatal effects of her disease, and our translators
have very properly rendered the Greek word *sōzō*, —
not saved as they have usually done, but — "healed,"
and this is the word (*khalam*) that is employed in the
Syriac.

The story of the woman who "was made whole,"
into which the above incident is interpolated by way
of episode, has already been noticed in Matt 9 : 21.

| 6: 56 And whithersoever He entered, into villages, or cities, or country, they laid the sick in the streets, and besought Him that they might touch if it were but the border of His garment: and as many as touched Him were made (*esōzōnto*) *whole.* | And all they that touched Him were *healed.* |

Here also our translators have very properly rendered the verb *sōzō*, "made whole," instead of, were
saved, as it is in the Greek; so it is *healed* in the
Syriac also.

10: 52 And Jesus said unto him, Go thy way; thy faith hath made thee (*sesōke*) *whole.* And immediately he received his sight, and followed Jesus in the way.

Thy faith hath procured thee LIFE.

Our English revision has rendered the Greek word *sōzō* " made whole," but the Syriac text reads, " hath procured thee Life." The restoration of his sight, or rather the cure of his blindness, was all this man asked or expected, but on account of his faith, our Lord gave him — as he often did to those who had faith in Him — more than he sought — even the Life of the Gospel.

It will be observed that hitherto we have found only the verb *sōzō,* " to save," or " to be saved," but in the cases that are to follow, we shall find the noun *Sōtēr,* which is translated " Savior" in our version, but which in the Syriac is LIFE–GIVER; and also the noun *sōtēria* which we translate " salvation," but which in the Syriac reads LIFE, the life which the Life-Giver bestows.

III. LUKE.

SYRIAC.

1: 47 And my spirit hath rejoiced in God my (*Sōtēri*) *Savior.*

My spirit is rejoicing in God my LIFE–GIVER.

This is a part of the " magnificat " of Mary on her visit to Elizabeth. Commenting on this, Holding says: " Could the doctrine of natural immortality and eternal pain have lived beside the constant joy of a people who sang of God having sent His Son into the world, ' that all men might *live* through Him'? Surely we have suffered much in the conception of the high meaning of the Gospel, by using ' Savior' instead of LIFE–GIVER. This word has for its root, *khya,* preceded by *mem,* the characteristic of the participle, and also used to form a noun from the verb, and then the possessive noun follows the root, ' my Life-Giver.' "

2

1: 69 And hath raised up an horn of (*sotērias*) *salvation* for us, in the house of His servant David.

And hath raised up a horn of *deliverance* for us in the house of David, His servant.

71 That we should be (*sotērian*) *saved* from our enemies, and from the hand of all that hate us;

That we should be *delivered* from our enemies.

77 To give knowledge of (*sotērias*) *salvation* unto His people, by the remission of their sins.

To give the knowledge of LIFE to His people, by the remission of their sins.

Here in the Greek, we have the word *Sotēria*, Salvation three times. In the first two cases, Zacharias evidently refers to a temporal or political deliverance — as it is rendered in our version — but in the last clause he speaks prophetically of the greater gift of LIFE through Christ. So in the Syriac, in the first two cases, we have *porkina, puraka*, words meaning simply *redemption* or *deliverance*, but in the last clause, the higher benefit — the gift of Life is plainly set forth by the word (*khya*) LIFE.

2: 11 For unto you is born this day, in the city of David, a (*Sotēr*) *Savior*, which is Christ the Lord.

For there is born to you, this day a *Deliverer* (*Paroka*) who is the Lord Messiah.

These are the words in which the angel announced to the Shepherds the birth of Christ. The Jews had now come under the Roman power and severely felt the humiliation, and the burden of the taxation that Cesar Augustus had begun to levy upon them. They were looking for the Deliverer or bond breaker that had been so long foretold by their prophets. This was the joyful news that was now made known to them, — that He had actually come, and was "this day born in Bethlehem." This was not intended to be a full declaration of His office and work. They were not yet ready for all this. They were told only just what was first in their thoughts and desires. So the term of highest signification, "Life-Giver," is not here found in the Syriac — the lower word (*Paroka*) Deliverer only is employed.

7: 50 And He said to the   Thy faith hath given thee
woman, Thy faith hath (*se-*   LIFE; go in peace.
sōke) *saved* thee; go in peace.

These are the cheering words of Jesus to the
" woman that was a sinner," who so kindly and peni-
tently ministered to Him in the house of Simon.
They are the very words He also addressed to the
woman whom He cured of the issue of blood, and to
the blind man, to whom He gave sight. (Matt. 9 : 22;
Mark 5 : 34.) They came to Him seeking only a
temporal benefit, and carried away, on account of
their faith, the infinitely higher blessing of ETERNAL
LIFE. This is shown by the use of the higher word
in the Syriac, but not in the Greek.

8: 12 Those by the way-   And taketh away the word
side, are they that hear; then   out of their heart, that they
cometh the devil, and taketh   may not believe and LIVE.
away the word out of their
hearts, lest they should believe and be (*sōzōsin*) *saved.*

Here again the Syriac, more clearly than the Greek,
shows what the salvation of the Gospel is, viz. : LIFE,
and how it is received through belief of the truth.
This is just what Satan would prevent.

Omitting several passages that have been considered in the foregoing Gospels, we next note :

13: 23 Then said one unto   And a person asked Him
Him, Lord, are there few that   whether there were few who
be (*sōzomenai*) *saved?*   would have LIFE.

This is a noteworthy passage, both on account of
the question asked, and the reply that our Lord made
to it. It is evident from the context, that this is not
a question simply of *rescue* from impending evil, but
of heirship in the everlasting kingdom, that Christ had
come to institute. For He goes on to tell those who
heard Him, that many shall seek to enter in and shall
not be able ; that they shall come from the East and
from the West, and from the North and the South,
and shall sit down in the kingdom — and they themselves shall be thrust out. So we have, not simply
saved, but LIFE in the Syriac.

17: 19 And He said unto him Arise; go thy way, thy faith hath (*sesōke*) *made thee whole.*

Arise, go, thy faith hath given thee LIFE.

This is a very unfortunate rendering in the English version ; and even in the Greek it is quite ambiguous. Our Lord had healed ten lepers, but only one of them turned back to give thanks, and to glorify God for the benefit conferred. To him our Lord replied that his faith had — surely not saved him or made him whole, as the Greek and English would seem to imply, in the sense of restoring him to health, but had — given him LIFE — the great Gospel blessing which it was Christ's special prerogative to confer — and was given only to those who exercised faith in Him. All these lepers had received the lower boon of restoration to health ; but only this one, the Samaritan had, through his faith, received the infinitely higher gift of LIFE at the hand of the LIFE–GIVER. So it reads in the Syriac, the very language in which Christ spoke, " Thy faith hath given thee LIFE."

19: 9 And Jesus said unto him, This day is (*sōtēria*) *salvation* come to this house, forasmuch as he also is a son of Abraham.

This day is LIFE to this house; for he also is a son of Abraham.

10 For the Son of man is come to seek and to (*sōzai*) *save* that which was lost.

For the Son of man came to seek and to impart LIFE to that which was lost.

Such was the result of our Lord's visit to the house of Zaccheus. He was a son of Abraham according to the flesh, for he was a Jew ; but this did not constitute him an heir of the kingdom of heaven. It was only by faith — the same that Abraham exercised, that he could receive the LIFE of that kingdom. This faith he showed by bringing forth fruits meet for repentance.

IV. JOHN.

SYRIAC.

3: 14 And as Moses lifted ▲
up the serpent in the wilder-
ness, even so must the Son
of man be lifted up:

15 That whosoever believ-
eth in Him should not perish,
but have eternal life.

16 For God so loved the
world, that He gave His only
begotten Son, that whoso-
ever believeth in Him, should
not perish, but have everlasting life.

17 For God sent not His
Son into the world to con-
demn the world, but that the
world through Him might
be (*sōthō*) saved.

That the world through
Him might Live.

This is one of the most important, among the many
very explicit passages in this Gospel, in its decisive
bearing on the doctrine of Eternal Life only through
Christ. That the full force of it, and the superiority
of the Syriac to the Greek reading may be the more
obvious, the two preceding verses have been cited to
be read in connection with it. Although the nature
of this salvation spoken of in verse seventeen, is
shown to be a salvation — not simply FROM sin and
misery, but exaltation TO Everlasting life, by the preceding verses, yet in the Syriac this is not left to be
inferred, but is emphatically declared: — That the
world through Him might have LIFE.

4: 22 For (*hē Sōtēria*) salvation is of the Jews.

For LIFE is from the Jews

This is the divinely appointed channel or medium
through which salvation was to come.

4: 42 And said unto the
woman, Now we believe, not
because of thy saying: for
we have heard Him ourselves,
and know that this is indeed
the Christ, the (*Sōtēr*) Savior
of the world.

We know that He is truly
the Messiah, the LIFE-GIVER
of the world.

The interview of Christ with the woman of Samaria, and with her fellow-townsman of Sychar, offers many interesting points for remark, bearing on this question of LIFE through Christ alone. I can notice only very briefly a few of them. The Samaritans were not Jews; but they were mainly Hebrews, with a large intermixture of other races, that had been imported into the country by their conquerors. Though widely alienated from the Judeans, in their worship, and in social life, they still retained the books of Moses, the traditions of the Hebrews, and their forms of worship. They were, like the Jews, looking for the Messiah, but evidently without any true conception of the spiritual nature of His mission. The gentle and effective way in which Jesus made Himself known to the woman at the well, as the Messiah, and enlightened her as to the true object of His mission, is very instructive. After exciting her surprise, by asking the gift of some water to drink, at her hands, He says: "If thou knewest the *Gift* of God, and who it is that saith to thee, Give me to drink, thou wouldst have asked Him, and He would have given thee living water"—that is, the Water of Life. Then, when, in her astonishment she inquires, if He is greater than Jacob, from whom the well had been received, He replies: "Whosoever drinketh of this water shall thirst again, but whosoever drinketh of the water that I shall give him, shall never thirst (will not thirst forever, *Syriac*), but the water that I shall give him, shall be in him a well of water springing up into Eternal Life."

Having had awakened, in her mind, some ill-defined desire for such a wonderful gift, and some imperfect conception of Him, as the Giver, she begins to inquire about the true place of worship — a question in dispute between the Samaritans and the Judeans. Our Lord replies (verse 22 above) that *the* salvation (notice the definite article *the*) is of the Jews. Olshausen thinks that by this term " the salvation," is meant, the one bringing salvation, the Savior, is not of the Samaritans, but of the Jews. The Syriac is still more explicit, for, instead of "the salvation," it reads *The Life*, or the LIFE-GIVER is of the Jews.

After receiving some further instruction concerning the spiritual nature of true worship, she says : " I know that the Messiah (which is called the Christ) when He cometh, will tell us all things." Note : The word Messiah is the Syriac word for " Anointed "; in the Greek it is " Christ." This parenthesis, explaining the meaning of the word Messiah, is not found in the Syriac —for it is not needed, — it has evidently been introduced by the Greek editors, and retained in our English version. And now the way having been fully prepared, Jesus declares Himself to be the Messiah. This is the first direct announcement He made to any one of Himself as the Messiah, the Christ, for whom the people were looking : and she, at once, as it would appear, believed on Him. And after her neighbors had been called, and had heard His words — for He remained two days with them — they too believed and said : " Now we know that He is truly the Messiah, the LIFE-GIVER of the world. It is difficult to perceive how any one can so read, or rather mis-read this narrative, whether in the Greek or in our English version, so as to see in Christ nothing more than a Savior from sin and misery, or at most, a Giver of pardon and purity and happiness to repenting sinners. But reading it in the Syriac it would seem to be utterly impossible for any one to take Him to be anything less than the actual GIVER of ETERNAL LIFE to perishing men.

5: 34 But I receive not testimony from man: but these things I say, that ye might be (*sōthēte*) *saved.*	But these things I say that ye may LIVE.

The chief topic of our Lord's discourse to the Jews, as recorded in this and the next following chapter, is *The Life Eternal* which God had provided for men, and which was now offered to them, through Himself, as the true Messiah. These words, though spoken on two different occasions, may be summarized as follows:

"1. That man has no principle of eternally enduring life in himself;

"2. That God has given us Eternal Life in His Son;

"3. That man's actual enjoyment of Eternal Life depends on the closest union with the Incarnate Life of God in Christ;

"4. That the Eternal Life bestowed on us includes and requires the immortality of the whole humanity, and therefore carries with it the Resurrection of the dead." (*Life in Christ*, p. 219.)

After asserting most emphatically His own divine authority and power to raise the dead and to give life to whomsoever He will, and that he who honoreth not the Son honoreth not the Father who sent Him, and that as the Father hath Life in Himself, so hath He given the Son to have Life in Himself, and he who heareth and believeth His words hath Everlasting Life and shall not come into condemnation — He says in reply to their murmurs — " These things I say that ye may LIVE. So it reads in the language in which He spoke to them. Why these words should be changed in the Greek, and consequently in our version so as to read " that ye might be saved," I know not, unless it be to afford some apology, under this ambiguous word, for the dogma of the Grecian philosophy, that was so early injected into the creed of the Christian church, that this salvation is simply a rescue of *immortal sinners* from an endless life of sin and misery, and a restoration to the love and favor of God, and to a state of blessedness that is also endless. Such indeed, is the popular understanding of this word " saved," at the present time. But any unprejudiced reader of these remarkable discourses especially in the Syriac, cannot fail to perceive how utterly inconsistent this doctrine is with the whole tenor of our Lord's teaching, from beginning to end. The sixth long chapter, throughout, is a continual reiteration under a variety of illustrations, of this one leading theme. And what was the result? The very same as when this great Gospel truth is preached at the present day — They were offended. " From that time many of His disciples went back, and walked no more with Him." And Jesus said to the Twelve, as all others were leaving Him, " Will ye also go away? Peter replied, Lord, to whom shall we go? Thou hast the words of Eternal Life."

Ah, men are willing enough to be told that Christ will *save* them from the consequences of their sins, if you will but grant them their favorite dogma of *Immortality* in their own right. If you will only flatter them with the notion that they have never forfeited this — that they cannot forfeit it by sin — just what the Tempter told Eve — they are quite willing to listen. But when you tell them that they have no Eternal Life in themselves — that they must receive it as a Gift from God by repentance and faith in Christ, or they will utterly perish — they are offended — they will turn away from such preaching, as they did from Christ, when he preached this doctrine.

"The doctrine of Immortality through the Incarnation, and of death eternal coming upon all men out of Christ, is the chief stumbling-block of the Gospel. It was the *last* truth for the church to learn, and the *first* for her to lose; — as it will be the last that she will consent to receive again by unlearning the notion which represents man's immortality as independent of Redemption." *Edward White.*

10: 9 I am the door: by me if any man enter in, he shall be (*sōthēsetai*) *saved*, and shall go in and out, and find pasture.

And if any man enter by me he will LIVE.

The superior reading of the Syriac is here seen, as in other cases, and is still further confirmed by the verses following: "I am come that they might have Life, and that they might have it" — not *more* abundantly as in our old version, but as it is in the revision — "abundantly," or in abundance, or as it is in the Syriac — "that life which is excellent." Our natural life is limited and transitory; the LIFE that Christ gives is unlimited and ever enduring.

11: 12 Then said His disciples, Lord, if he sleep, he shall (*sōthēsetai*) *do well.*

Lord, if he sleepeth, he is *recovering.*

This was the reply made by the disciples to our Lord, when He had said to them, "Our friend Lazarus sleepeth, but I go that I may awake him out of sleep."

2*

The English rendering, " He shall do well," is better than the Greek, " He shall be saved," and so it reads in the Syriac, " He is recovering." For reference is here, not to the salvation of the Gospel, but to the recovery of his health; hence the higher word (*Khya*), LIFE, is not employed, but the lower word, implying deliverance; for the two ideas are always kept distinct in the Syriac.

12: 27 Now is my soul troubled; and what shall I say? Father, (*sōzon*) *save* me from this hour: but for this cause came I unto this hour.	And what shall I say? My Father, *deliver* me from this hour? But for this cause came I to this hour.

The second clause in the above verse is to be read as an interrogation, as well as the first, as it is in the Syriac. Christ naturally shrinks from the dreadful death to which He is consciously hastening, and He inquires, shall I ask to be saved from it? — and immediately answers in the negative His own inquiry; " *No* " — " For this very purpose have I come." It is not a question of life simply, much less of the Life of the Gospel, but of a Salvation or rescue from the dreadful experience that awaits Him. He submissively resigns Himself even to this, because it is the will of the Father, and the very object for which He had been sent into the world, — to give His own life for the redemption of the world. The superiority of the Syriac to the Greek, in consistency and clearness, must be evident to every one.

12: 47 And if any man hear my words, and believe not, I judge him not: for I came not to judge the world, but to (*sōsō*) *save* the world.	But to give LIFE to the world (or vivify it).

This is the last occurrence of this word *sōzō* in this Gospel. It is almost identical with the first (3: 17). It needs no further comment. It is to be remarked that LIFE, ETERNAL LIFE, through Christ and through Him alone, is the great leading theme of this Gospel. It is partly obscured in our version and in the Greek, which we have followed by the use of the words

"Save," "Savior," "Salvation," when the words *Sōzō,
Sōtēr* and *Sōtēria* occur in the Greek; but still, it
stands out so prominently in the word *zōē; zōē aiōnios;
hē zōē aiōnios*, Life, Life Everlasting, the Life Everlasting, — repeated as it is, thirty-six times in this
Gospel, and seventeen times in the other three Gospels, that it would seem to be impossible for any one
to misapprehend it. It was the very first thought in
the intercessory prayer of our Lord on the night
before His crucifixion.

"These words spake Jesus and lifted up His eyes to
heaven and said: Father, glorify thy Son, that thy Son may
also glorify thee: as thou hast given Him power over all
flesh, that He should give ETERNAL LIFE, to as many as
thou hast given Him. And this is Eternal Life, that they
might know thee, the only true God, and Jesus Christ whom
thou hast sent."

John, the writer of this Gospel, is so impressed
with it, that he carries it into his chief Epistle, and
makes it the leading thought there, and gives this
emphatic record in the closing words of the Epistle :

"This is the Record that God hath given to us Eternal
Life, and this Life is in His Son. He that hath the Son,
hath Life, and he that hath not the Son, hath not Life."

V. ACTS.

In this book — undoubtedly written by Luke the
writer of the third Gospel, — the same superiority of
the Syriac to the Greek in expressing more explicitly
the ideas which are translated "save," "Savior,"
"salvation," is apparent. It will not be important to
cite every case.

	SYRIAC.
2: 21 And it shall come to pass, that whosoever shall call on the name of the Lord, shall be (*sōthēsetai*) *saved.*	And it shall be, that who-ever shall call on the name of the Lord shall LIVE.
2: 47 Praising God. and having favor with all the people. And the Lord added to the church daily such as should be (*sōzomenous*) *saved.*	And the Lord was gather-ing every day those who had partaken of . LIFE into the church.

The former of these two passages is a part of Peter's address on the day of Pentecost; the latter gives the result of the outpouring of the Spirit on that day; in both of which the nature of the salvation spoken of is unmistakably described in the Syriac. It is not a temporal salvation, but one that is spiritual and Eternal; it is not merely a salvation *from* sin and misery, but also a salvation *to* Life; and those who had become partakers of this new Life were gathered into the church. Would that only such now, and always, were gathered into the church!

4: 9 If we this day be examined of the good deed done to the impotent man; by what means he is made (*se̮ōtai*) *whole.*	By what means he was *healed.*
4: 12 Neither is there (*sō-tĕria*) *salvation* in any other: for there is none other name under heaven given among men, whereby we must (*sō-thēnai*) *be saved.*	Neither is there deliverance (or redemption from death) in any other, for there is not another name under heaven which is given to men whereby to Live.

In this narrative of the restoration of the impotent man, and Peter's defence of himself for his agency in the matter, the Greek words *save* and *salvation* occur three times. In the first instance it is very properly rendered in our version (not saved, but) "made whole," for he is speaking of the temporal or bodily cure of this man. But Peter now takes occasion to proclaim in the unwilling ears of these priests and rulers, the higher truth of the Gospel. Hence the radical distinction between the lower and higher blessing, both of which are indeed from the same source, though the difference between them is not indicated in the Greek or English, but it is conspicuously brought out in the Syriac, by words that are radically distinct.

5: 31 Him hath God exalted with His right hand to be a Prince and a (*Sōtĕra*) *Savior,* for to give repentance to Israel, and forgiveness of sins.	Him hath God exalted with His own right hand to be a Prince and Life-Giver, for to give repentance and forgiveness of sins to Israel.

This is a part of Peter's bold speech before the San-
hedrim after his miraculous deliverance from prison,
into which he had been cast with the other Apostles.
The angel that delivered them, told them to go and
speak all the words of (*tēs zōēs tautēs*) this Life, and
they went into the temple and began to preach as they
had been bidden. And when the officers, the next
morning, failing, to their astonishment, to find them
in the prison, and to their greater astonishment, found
them preaching the Word of Life, in the temple, they
took them without violence, fearing the people, and
brought them again before the council to answer for
their disobedience. Then Peter addressed them in
the words quoted above (see context 29–32 verses).

"How fitting that Peter should call Him a 'Life-Giver,'
both in view of what the angel who opened the prison doors
bid the Apostles do, and also in view of his former words to
the same council as noticed above (see 4: 12). It was Syriac
or Syro-Chaldaic that Peter spoke, and no doubt but he used
not *Sōtēr*, the Greek word for Savior, but *Makhyna*, Life-
Giver. Now how fitly one who knows the preaching of
Christ to be a message of Life, calls its great Subject the
LIFE-GIVER." (*Holding.*)

7: 25 For he supposed his brethren would have under-stood how that God by his hand would (*sōtērian, deliver-ance*) *deliver* them: but they understood not.

That by his hand would give them *deliverance.*

Stephen is here speaking of deliverance from their
bondage in Egypt, and not of the salvation of the
Gospel — certainly not of the boon of Eternal Life —
and so the word *sōtēria* is very properly rendered, "to
deliver," or "deliverance," in our version. So it is
also expressed in the Syriac.

11: 14 Who shall tell thee words, whereby thou and all thy house (*sōthēsē*) *shall be saved.*

Words by which thou shalt LIVE.

Peter is here giving an account of his mission to
Cornelius, and what the angel had said of him to
Cornelius. We learn from the Syriac what sort of
salvation is meant, and what is necessary to it. In

commenting on this passage, it has been well said by
the author just cited :

"If a company of modern teachers, whose reputation as
leading men stands high, had sat in judgment on the question of character, as set forth in Luke's account of Cornelius,
they would have decided that he was all right. Mark the
points of excellence as briefly sketched by the historian.
(1) He was a devout man (*Syriac* righteous man). (2) He
was one who feared God. (3) He, like Abraham, taught
all his house, children and servants to do the same, and suc-
ceeded.   (4) He did many righteous things among the
people. He gave much alms, or showed active benevolence.
(5) He prayed at all times. Surely, such a. man was one
whom neither minister, apostle, nor angel need feel any
concern about. But whatever men might have decided
about Cornelius, God did not deem him safe without more
light from Gospel teaching. And hence, an angel was sent
to tell him what to do. And what he must do is to send for
Peter who could preach to him, and his household words,
by which they might lay hold on Life."

Do not the Scriptures here teach us very plainly,
that, no matter how moral a man may be — whether
in heathen or in Christian lands, — he needs to know
Christ and His Gospel in order to Salvation unto Eternal Life ? "How shall they believe in Him of whom
they have not heard? How shall they hear without a
preacher ? and how shall they preach except they be
sent?"   And when they (the objectors at Jerusalem),
heard these things, they held their peace, and glorified
God, saying : "Then hath God also, to the Gentiles
granted repentance unto (*zŏēn*) Life."

13: 23 Of this man's seed
hath God, according to His
promise, raised unto Israel a
(*Sŏtēra*) Savior, Jesus:

God hath raised up to
Israel, as He hath promised,
Jesus, a *Deliverer.*

13: 26 Men and brethren,
children of the stock of Abraham, and whosoever among
you feareth God, to you is
the word of this (*Sŏtērias*)
Salvation sent.

To you is this word of LIFE
sent.

We have in this chapter an account of what Paul
and Barnabas said to the Jews at Antioch (Pisidia)
when they showed themselves unworthy of the Life
that was offered them, and of the effect of their
preaching to the Gentiles of that city.

Paul begins his address to the Jews, not by speaking at once of Christ in the higher sense, as the Giver of LIFE, — but not to offend their prejudices, he first speaks of Him, simply as a Deliverer — as is evident from the Syriac (verse 23). Then after having gained their favorable attention, he goes on to say more explicitly, " To you is this word of LIFE sent." The Gentile part of his audience seem to have been especially impressed by his address on the first Sabbath; and so, after the Jews had retired, they requested that this truth might be further expounded to them on the next Sabbath. This excited the envy of the Jews, and stirred them up to violent opposition. " On the next Sabbath, almost the whole city came together to hear the word of God." There was great excitement. The Jews turned against the Apostles, " and spoke against those things which were spoken by Paul, contradicting and blaspheming."

13: 46 Then Paul and Barnabas waxed bold, and said, It was necessary that the word of God should first have been spoken to you: but seeing ye put it from you, and judge yourselves unworthy of Everlasting Life, lo, we turn to the Gentiles:	But because ye repel it from you, and decide against yourselves, that ye are not worthy of Life Eternal, lo, we turn ourselves to the Gentiles.
47 For so hath the Lord commanded us, saying, I have set thee to be a light of the Gentiles, that thou shouldest be for (*sōtērian*) *salvation* unto the ends of the earth.	For so hath our Lord commanded us as it is written, I have set thee a light to the Gentiles, that thou shouldest be for LIFE unto the ends of the earth.

Here we have — instead of *Sōtērian*, Salvation, as it is in the Greek and English — the higher and more definite word LIFE in the Syriac, and this, it will be seen, agrees with what had just been said of " Everlasting Life " in verse 46.

After their return to Antioch (Syria), a controversy springs up in the church with respect to imposing the Jewish rite of circumcision on the Gentile converts. Some Jewish Christians from Jerusalem had taught them, saying:

15: 1 Except ye be cir-
cumcised after the manner
of Moses, ye cannot be (*sōthēnai*) *saved*.

Except ye be circumcised,
ye cannot have LIFE.

So a delegation was sent down to Jerusalem to
inquire of the church there, "about this question."
After much controversy, Peter closed the discussion,
in a very catholic and liberal speech which concludes
with these words :

15: 11 But we believe,
that through the grace of the
Lord Jesus Christ, we shall
be (*sōthēnai*) *saved*, even as
they.

We believe that we, as well
as they, are to have LIFE, by
the grace of the Lord Jesus
Messiah.

Now in both of the above passages, instead of
sōthēnai, to be saved, as it is in Greek and English, we have in the Syriac the more explicit word,
"have Life," showing what is meant by being saved.

16: 17, 30, 31. The incidents of this sixteenth
chapter suggest many interesting topics for remark,
but we must confine our attention to the one point in
hand. The Greek noun *sōtēria*, salvation, occurs once
in verse seventeen, and the verb *sōzō*, to save, occurs
twice in the thirtieth and thirty-first verses, under the
following circumstances. Paul and Silas, in their missionary tour, were now at Philippi. Here they were
followed from day to day by a noisy damsel, a Pytho-
ness, who continually cried, saying :

16: 17 These men are the
servants of the Most High
God, which shew unto us the
way of (*Sōtērias*) *Salvation*.

They announce to you the
way of LIFE.

The apostles were unwilling to receive any patron-
izing testimony from such a source. And so, after
suffering this for many days — following their Mas-
ter's example, who rebuked the devils when they
cried, saying, "Thou art Christ, the Son of God"
(Luke 4: 4) — they turned and exorcised the spirit
that possessed her. By doing this, they brought down
on themselves the wrath of her masters, whose gain,
by her soothsaying, was now at an end. The consequence was, they were cruelly beaten, and then cast

into the inner prison, and their feet were made fast in the stocks. There, in their dark cavern, at midnight, while, in spite of their sufferings, they were singing praises to God, " suddenly there was a great earthquake, so that the foundations of the prison were shaken, and immediately all the doors were opened, and every one's bands were loosed." The jailer, who was responsible with his own life for the safe keeping of his charge, in the terror of the moment was about to do, what many men have done, to commit suicide — hoping to escape from present evils by flying to others we know not of, just what Brutus and Cassius did in this very city of Philippi, — when Paul interposed to prevent him. After he had become assured of the safety of his prisoners, and had had time for reflection, better thoughts took possession of his mind. He thought of the character of these two men, and of what the damsel had said, " They teach the people the way of LIFE." Perhaps he had heard the message from their own lips. He thought of their unjust and cruel treatment, and of their wonderful demeanor through it all ; and of the miraculous interposition of heaven in their behalf. Sudden conviction seizes him. He trembles before these servants of God, as in the presence of God Himself. His only thought now, in this midnight hour, is not of the concerns of this life, but of the Life to come. " Then he called for a light, and sprang in, and came trembling, and fell down before Paul and Silas : "

16: 30 And brought them out, and said, Sirs, what must I do to be (*sōthō*) *saved ?*	My lords, what must I do that I may have LIFE?
31 And they said, Believe on the Lord Jesus Christ, and thou shalt (*sōthēsē*) *be saved,* and thy house.	And they said to him, Believe on the name of our Lord Jesus Messiah, and thou wilt have LIFE, thou and thy house.

The mission of Paul and Silas to these Philippians was not to proclaim any temporal salvation, nor mere salvation of any kind, as many interpret the Gospel, but LIFE, *Eternal Life*, through Jesus Christ. The damsel correctly characterized it as " The Way of

Life." So the people understood it. So did the jailer. Hence, he did not simply ask, as might be inferred from our version, and from the Greek — what must I do to be saved? but "What must I do that I may have Life?" that LIFE through Christ which you have come to announce. And their reply is equally explicit, "Believe on the name of our Lord Jesus Messiah, and thou wilt have LIFE, thou and thy house." Every one must observe how much more explicit is the Syriac than the Greek and English, in this case as well as in the many others that have been already noticed.

There are several other cases in this book, for instance, in Chapter 27: 20, 32, 34, where the words evidently refer to salvation in its lower and physical sense; but as there is nothing peculiar in these cases, we need not stop to give them particular notice.

VI. THE PAULINE EPISTLES.

The cases where the Greek words *Sōzō*, *Sōtēr*, and *Sōtēria*, occur in these epistles, are so numerous, and we have commented so freely upon similar cases already, that we must now deal with them in a more summary manner. This we can well do; for the same principle and method of rendering are carried through the whole of the New Testament; namely: whenever temporal or physical salvation is in question, or deliverance of any sort, the Syriac uses such words as imply *rescue, cure, release, deliver*, etc. But where the peculiar gift of the Gospel through Christ is evidently spoken of, the words signifying to *Live, Life*, the *Life-Giver*, are always employed to designate it. But on the other hand, in the Greek, no such distinction is made; nor is it often made in our English version, which follows the Greek.

ROMANS.

There are eleven cases in this epistle. They may all be grouped together, the rendering from the Greek and the Syriac side by side, without remark, and the reader can make the comparison for himself.

SYRIAC.

1: 16 For I am not ashamed of the Gospel of Christ: for it is the power of God unto (*Sōtērian*) *Salvation* to every one that believeth; to the Jew first, and also to the Greek.

For I am not ashamed of the Gospel ["of Christ" omitted in the Syriac], for it is the power of God unto LIFE, to all who believe it.

5: 9 Much more then, being now justified by His blood, we shall be (*sōthēsometha*) *saved* from wrath through Him.

How much more shall we now be justified by His blood, and be *rescued* from wrath by Him?

10 For if when we were enemies, we were reconciled to God by the death of His Son; much more, being reconciled, we shall (*sōthēsometha*) *be saved* by His life.

For if when we were enemies, God was reconciled with us by the death of His Son, how much more shall we in His reconciliation LIVE by His life.

8: 24 For we are (*esōthēmen*) *saved* by hope.

Because we LIVE by hope (or in hope).

9: 27 Esaias also crieth concerning Israel, Though the number of the children of Israel be as the sand of the sea, a remnant shall be (*sōthēsetai*) *saved*.

A remnant of them will LIVE.

10: 1 Brethren, my heart's desire and prayer to God for Israel is, that they might be (*eis sōtērian*) *saved*.

That they might LIVE.

9 That if thou shalt confess with thy mouth the Lord Jesus, and shalt believe in thine heart that God hath raised Him from the dead, thou shalt be (*sōthēsē*) *saved*.

Thou shalt LIVE.

10 For with the heart, man believeth unto righteousness; and with the mouth, confession is made unto (*Sōtērian*) *Salvation*.

The mouth that confesseth Him is restored to LIFE.

11: 11 I say then, Have they stumbled that they should fall? God forbid: but rather through their fall (*Sōtēria*) *Salvation* is come unto the Gentiles.

By their stumbling, Life hath come to the Gentiles.

14 If by any means I may provoke to emulation them which are my flesh, and might (*sōsō*)*save* some of them.

Might Vivify (or give life to) some of them.

26 And so all Israel shall be (*sōthēsetai*) *saved*.

And then all Israel will Live.

13: 11 And that, knowing the time, that now it is high time to awake out of sleep: for now is our (*Sōtēria*) *Salvation* nearer than when we believed.

For now our Life hath come nearer to us than when we believed.

I. CORINTHIANS.

In this epistle there are thirteen cases, all of the Greek verb *sōzō*, to save, and all but one, referring to the Gospel gift of Life, are represented in the Syriac by (*Khya*, the root word for) Life.

SYRIAC.

1: 18 For the preaching of the cross is to them that perish, foolishness; but unto us which are (*sōzomenois*) *saved*, it is the power of God.

But to us who Live it is the energy of God.

21 For after that in the wisdom of God the world by wisdom knew not God, it pleased God by the foolishness of preaching to (*sōsai*) *save* them that believe.

To Quicken (or to cause to live) them who believe.

3: 15 If any man's work shall be burned, he shall suffer loss: but he himself shall be (*sōthēsetai*) *saved*; yet so as by fire.

But he himself will *escape*, but it will be as from the fire.

Here the thought is fixed, not on what is gained but on what is avoided or escaped, and so instead of Live we very significantly have (*Shazab*) escape.

5: 5 To deliver such an one unto Satan for the destruction of the flesh, that the spirit may (*sōthē*) *be saved* in the day of the Lord Jesus.

For the destruction of the body, that in the spirit, he may have LIFE in the day of our Lord Jesus Messiah.

This passage raises a perplexing question. I know not how to put any other interpretation on it than what lies on the surface. Reference is here made to what is said in the verse next, above quoted, (15 verse) and to the two following, 16 and 17 verses, in which the body is declared to be the temple of God. The merciful result of this severe church discipline is seen in Paul's second Epistle to this Church, 2: 5-10.

7: 16 For what knowest thou, O wife, whether thou shalt (*sōseis*) *save* thy husband? or how knowest thou, O man, whether thou shalt (*sōseis*) *save* thy wife?

— Procure LIFE to thy husband. — Procure LIFE to thy wife.

9: 22 To the weak became I as weak, that I might gain the weak: I am made all things to all men, that I might by all means (*sōsō*) *save* some.

That I might bring LIFE to every one.

We are taught here the hard lesson of yielding up everything in the way of personal preference or convenience — everything but principle — to the prejudices and weaknesses of our fellow-men, in order to win them to Christ. This thought is repeated in our next citation.

10: 33 Even as I please all men in all things, not seeking mine own profit, but the profit of many, that they may (*sōthōsi*) *be saved.*

That they may LIVE.

15: 2 By which also ye (*sōzesthe*) *are saved*, if ye keep in memory what I preached unto you, unless ye have believed in vain.

By which ye have LIFE.

II. CORINTHIANS.

1: 6 And whether we be afflicted, it is for your consolation and salvation, which is effectual in the enduring of the same sufferings which we also suffer: or whether we be comforted, it is for your consolation and (*Sōtērias*) *Salvation.*

It is for your consolation and your LIFE that we are afflicted.

The word *Sōtērias*, salvation, occurs twice in the Greek in this verse, and is so translated in our old version, but only once in the revised version, and this is in accordance with the Syriac.

6: 2 (For He saith, I have heard thee in a time accepted, and in the day of (*Sōtērias*) *Salvation* have I succored thee: behold, now is the accepted time; behold, now is the day of (*Sōtērias*) *Salvation.*)

In the day of LIFE have I aided thee. — Behold now is the day of LIFE.

7: 10 For godly sorrow worketh repentance to (*Sō-tērian*) *Salvation* not to be repented of: but the sorrow of the world worketh death.

For sorrowing on account of God, worketh a conversion of the soul, which is not reversed, and a turning unto LIFE.

The radical and permanent nature of true repentance is much more distinctly brought out in the Syriac than in the Greek and English readings.

In the Epistle to the GALATIANS there are no cases; and in the Epistle to the EPHESIANS there are only two or three; but as they bring nothing new to the question we are considering, they may be left without further notice; and pass on to the next Epistle, where there are three cases of *Sōtēria*, and one of *Sōtēr*, which it may be well to cite.

PHILIPPIANS.

1: 19 For I know that this shall turn to my (*Sōtē-rian*) *Salvation* through your prayer, and the supply of the Spirit of Jesus Christ.

For I know that these things will be found (conducive) to my LIFE.

Paul writes this letter while in prison at Rome, awaiting the issue of his trial. It may be thought that he here refers to the salvation of his natural life. In that case, the lower term in the Syriac, signifying deliverance, would have been appropriate; but as the higher term (*Khya*) LIFE is employed, it is to be understood in the Gospel sense, and is appropriately rendered "Life."

1: 28 And in nothing terrified by your adversaries: which is to them an evident token of perdition, but to you of (*Sōtērias*) *Salvation,* and that of God.

An indication of their de struction and of LIFE to you

2: 12 Wherefore, my beloved, as ye have always obeyed, not as in my presence only, but now much more in my absence, work out your own (*Sōtērian*) *Salvation* with fear and trembling.

Prosecute the work of your LIFE. (*Murdock.*)
Serve the service of your LIFE. (*Holding.*)

Although the Divine Life is a pure "gift," and not a reward of merit, this Life is to be cultivated by the diligent and faithful use of the means of grace.

3: 20 For our conversation is in heaven; from whence also we look for the (*Sōtēr*) *Savior,* the Lord Jesus Christ:

But our concern is in tho heaven; from thence we expect our LIFE-GIVER, our Lord Jesus the Messiah.

21 Who shall change our vile body, that it may be fashioned like unto His glorious body, according to the working whereby He is able even to subdue all things unto Himself.

When this passage is read in connection with the next following (21 verse, which we have also quoted above) referring to the doctrine of the Resurrection, and the change which our corruptible bodies are then to undergo, through the almighty power of this LIFE-GIVER, we see how much more clearly this term sets Him forth as "the Resurrection and the Life."

In the Epistle to the COLOSSIANS there are no cases to be noticed.

I. THESSALONIANS.

2: 16 Forbidding us to speak to the Gentiles that they might be (*sōthōsin*)*saved*.

That they may have LIFE.

The Jews regarded themselves as the special and exclusive favorites of heaven. Even those who had embraced Christianity could scarcely tolerate the idea of receiving Gentile converts to the same privileges with themselves under the Gospel.

5: 8 But let us, who are of the day, be sober, putting on the breastplate of faith and love; and for an helmet, the hope of (*Sōtērias*) *Salvation*.

And take the helmet of the hope of LIFE;

9 For God hath not appointed us to wrath, but to obtain (*Sōtērias*) *Salvation* by our Lord Jesus Christ.

For God hath not appointed us to wrath, but to the acquisition of LIFE, by our Lord Jesus the Messiah.

II. THESSALONIANS.

2: 10 And with all deceivableness of unrighteousness in them that perish; because they received not the love of the truth, that they might be (*sōthōnai*) *saved*.

By which they might have LIFE.

13 But we are bound to give thanks always to God for you, brethren beloved of the Lord, because God hath from the beginning chosen you to (*Sōtērian*) *Salvation*, through sanctification of the Spirit.

Chosen you unto LIFE.

I. TIMOTHY.

1: 1 Paul, an Apostle of Jesus Christ by the commandment of God our (*Sōtēros*) *Savior*, and Lord Jesus Christ, which is our hope;

By the command of Jesus our (*Mahynin*) LIFE-GIVER, and of the Messiah, Jesus our Hope.

15 This is a faithful saying, and worthy of all acceptation, that Christ Jesus came into the world to (*sōsai*) *save* sinners; of whom I am chief.

Jesus the Messiah came into the world to give LIFE to sinners.

2: 3 For this is good and acceptable in the sight of God our (*Sōtēros*) *Savior;*

For this is good and acceptable before God our LIFE-GIVER:

4 Who will have all men to be (*sōthēnai*) *saved*, and to come unto the knowledge of the truth.

Who would have all men LIVE and be converted to the knowledge of the truth.

4: 10 For therefore we both labor and suffer reproach, because we trust in the living God who is the (*Sōtēr*) *Savior* of all men, especially of those that believe.

Who is the LIFE-GIVER of all men, especially of believers.

The Living God has given life to all who live; for He is the Source of all life; but He is the LIFE-GIVER, in a special sense, of those who believe, even the Life that is Eternal.

II. TIMOTHY.

SYRIAC.

1: 9 Who hath (*sōsantos*) *saved* us, and called us with an holy calling.

Who hath given us LIFE, and called us with a holy calling.

2: 10 Therefore I endure all things for the elect's sake, that they may also obtain the (*Sōtērias*) *Salvation* which is in Christ Jesus with eternal glory.

That they may obtain LIFE, which is in Jesus the Messiah, with eternal glory.

3: 15 And that from a child thou hast known the Holy Scriptures, which are able to make thee wise unto (*Sōtērias*) *Salvation* through faith which is in Christ Jesus.

The holy books which can make thee wise unto LIFE.

4: 18 And the Lord shall deliver me from every evil work, and will (*sōsei*) *preserve* me unto His heavenly kingdom; to whom be glory for ever and ever. Amen.

And the Lord will *rescue* me from every evil work and give me LIFE in His heavenly kingdom.

3

Here, as elsewhere, the Syriac makes clear the broad distinction, which is not manifest in the Greek or English, between a *rescue* from evil, and the gift of the heavenly LIFE in the kingdom of Jesus Christ.

TITUS.

	SYRIAC.
1: 3 But hath in due times manifested His word through preaching, which is committed unto me, according to the commandment of God our (*Sōtēros*) *Savior*.	By the command of God our LIFE-GIVER.
4 To Titus, mine own son after the common faith: Grace, mercy, and peace, from God the Father, and the Lord Jesus Christ our (*Sōtēros*) *Savior*.	Grace and peace from God our Father, and from our Lord Jesus the Messiah our LIFE-GIVER.

The term "Life-Giver" is accorded to both the Father and the Son, for it is the gift of God through His Son Jesus Christ.

2: 10 Not purloining, but shewing all good fidelity; that they may adorn the doctrine of God our (*Sōtēros*) *Savior* in all things.	Of God our LIFE-GIVER in all things.
11 For the grace of God that bringeth (*Sōtērios*) *Salvation* hath appeared to all men.	For the all VIVIFYING (life-giving) grace of God is revealed to all men.
13 Looking for that blessed hope, and the glorious appearing of the great God and our (*Sōtēros*) *Savior* Jesus Christ;	Looking for the blessed hope and the manifestation of the glory of the great God our LIFE-GIVER, Jesus the Messiah.
3: 4 But after that the kindness and love of God our (*Sōtēros*) *Savior* toward man appeared.	But when the kindness and compassion of God our LIFE-GIVER was revealed,
5 Not by works of righteousness which we have done, but according to His mercy He (*esōsen*) *saved* us, by the washing of regeneration, and renewing of the Holy Ghost;	Not by works of righteousness which we have done, but by His mercy He QUICK-ENED us, by the washing of the new birth and by the renovation of the Holy Spirit,
6 Which he shed on us abundantly, through Jesus Christ our (*Sōtēros*) *Savior*;	which he shed on us richly by Jesus the Messiah our LIFE-GIVER.

VII. HEBREWS.

The Epistle to the Hebrews could hardly have been written by Paul, for various reasons, which we cannot now stop to consider, — though it might have been written by his associate Silas; and this is quite probable. That it was originally written in Syriac, like the Gospel of Matthew, and then translated into Greek, whatever may be true of the other Epistles, is generally admitted by the best critics. It gives us two cases of the verb *Sōzō*, and seven of the noun *Sōtēria*, all but one of which refer to the heavenly Life, and are so indicated in the Syriac by the use of the (root) word *Khya*.

	SYRIAC.
1: 14 Are they not all ministering spirits sent forth to minister for them who shall be heirs of (*Sōtērian*) *Salvation?*	To them who are to inherit LIFE.
2: 3 How shall we escape, if we neglect so great (*Sōtērias*) *Salvation*;	If we despise the things which are our LIFE.
10 For it became Him, for whom are all things, and by whom are all things, in bringing many sons unto glory, to make the Captain of their (*Sōtērias*) *Salvation* perfect through sufferings.	To perfect the Prince of their LIFE by suffering.
5: 7 Who in the days of His flesh, when He had offered up prayers and supplications with strong crying and tears unto Him that was able to (*sōzein*) *save* Him from death, and was heard in that He feared;	To Him who was able to RESUSCITATE Him from death, and He was heard.
9 And being made perfect, He became the Author of eternal (*Sōtērias*) *Salvation* unto all them that obey Him.	And thus He was perfected, and became the cause of Eternal LIFE to all them who obey Him. (The ladder of the Life which is Everlasting. *Holding.*)

The reference in verse 7 is to Christ's agony in the garden. It has commonly been regarded as a very

difficult passage. Commentators have stumbled over
it because they have construed the Greek verb *to save,*
as meaning to hinder, or prevent, to save him from
dying. But the Syriac reading to *resuscitate,* or to
raise again to life from death, makes the meaning perfectly clear. We know that He was heard in regard
to this very thing, — the restoration of His life after
death. For we are told, 2 Cor. 13: 4, "For though
He was crucified through weakness, yet He liveth by
the power of God." Eph. 1: 19. "According to the
working of His (God's) mighty power which He
wrought in Christ when *He raised Him from the dead.*

6: 9 But, beloved, we are persuaded better things of you, and things that accompany (*Sōtērias*) *Salvation,* though we thus speak.	Things which pertain to LIFE.
7: 25 Wherefore He is able also to (*sōzein*) *save* them to the uttermost that come unto God by Him, seeing He ever liveth to make interces- sion for them.	He is able to give LIFE for- ever to them who come to God by Him. For He always liveth and sendeth up prayers for them.
9: 28 So Christ was once offered to bear the sins of many; and unto them that look for Him shall He appear the second time without sin unto (*Sōtērian*) *Salvation.*	A second time, without sin, will He appear for the LIFE of those who expect Him.

His first Advent was to make an atonement for sin,
but His second Advent will have no such purpose.
It will be to receive His people into that Eternal LIFE
for which they are looking.

11: 7 By faith Noah, being warned of God of things not seen as yet, moved with fear, prepared an ark to the (*sōtē- rian*) *saving* of his house.	He made himself an ark for the LIFE of his household.

This last example is the only one of the nine in this
Epistle in which the word "save" in Greek, and
"Life" in Syriac, does not evidently have prime reference to the life of the world to come. Perhaps,
however, even here, both sorts of life should be in-

cluded under the one term "Life." This was an act of faith — and the salvation should not be understood as restricted to this life only.

VIII. THE CATHOLIC EPISTLES OF JAMES, PETER, AND JOHN.

JAMES.

SYRIAC.

1: 21 Wherefore lay apart all filthiness, and superfluity of naughtiness, and receive with meekness the ingrafted word, which is able to (*sōsai*) *save* your souls.

Which is able to give LIFE to your souls.

2: 14 What doth it profit, my brethren, though a man say he hath faith and have not works? can faith (*sōsai*) *save* him?

Can his faith give him LIFE?

4: 12 There is one Lawgiver, who is able to (*sōsai*) *save*, and to destroy.

Who can make ALIVE and can destroy.

5: 20 Let him know that he which converteth the sinner from the error of his way shall (*sōsei*) *save* a soul from death, and shall hide a multitude of sins.

Will RESUSCITATE a soul from death and cover the multitude of sins.

I. PETER.

SYRIAC.

1: 5 Who are kept by the power of God through faith unto (*Sōtērian*) *Salvation*, ready to be revealed in the last time.

Kept by the power of God and by faith for the LIFE that is prepared, and will be revealed in the last time.

9 Receiving the end of your faith, even the (*Sōtērian*) *Salvation* of your souls.

That ye may receive the recompense of your faith, the LIFE of your souls.

10 Of which (*Sōtērias*) *Salvation* the prophets have inquired and searched diligently, who prophesied of the grace that should come unto you.

That LIFE about which the prophets inquired, when they were prophesying of the grace which was to be given to you.

The Old Testament saints unquestionably had some true ideas of that future Life immortal — that "length of days forever and ever," which it was the purpose of God to give to His people, by a Resurrection from the dead. They prophesied of it, and warned sinners against the second death, from which there was no recovery, saying: " Why will ye die?" But it was only through types and figures and vague promises that this great doctrine was assured to them. Their faith laid hold of it as that "some better thing," that was yet to be more clearly revealed to His people. They did not, indeed, fully comprehend these promises, as we now read them in the Gospel, through which this " Life and Immortality are brought to light." They did not, indeed, comprehend the full import of their own prophecies, as we now comprehend them, but they searched diligently, that they might know them.

How happy are our ears,
That hear this joyful sound,
Which kings and prophets waited for,
And sought, but never found.

How blessed are our eyes,
That see this heavenly light;
Prophets and kings desired it long,
But died without the sight.

4: 18 And if the righteous scarcely be (*sōzetai*) *saved*, where shall the ungodly and the sinner appear?

If the righteous scarcely LIVETH, where will the ungodly and the sinner be found ?

I. JOHN.

4: 14 And we have seen and do testify that the Father sent the Son to be the (*Sōtēra*) *Savior* of the world.

We have seen and do testify that the Father hath sent His Son a *Redeemer* (*Prooka* or *Paroka*), for the world.

This passage last cited, and the last to be cited, is one of the most important of them all. It is only in the Syriac that the distinction is made clear between the Redemption of all the children of Adam, *from* their natural or Adamic death, by the death of Christ, and their salvation *to* Eternal Life. The word *Sōtēr* in Greek, always rendered *Savior* in English, usually reads LIFE-GIVER in the Syriac, because it is His chief prerogative to give the boon of Eternal Life to those who believe on Him. But here in the Syriac it does not read LIFE-GIVER, but *Redeemer*, for He is indeed the Redeemer of the world, the whole world. Redemption by Christ is as broad as our death by Adam. "As in Adam all die, so in Christ shall all be made alive." But this does not entitle all men to ETERNAL LIFE; it only brings them before the bar of God to answer for their own individual sins. It is only the righteous that enter into ETERNAL LIFE — the wicked are condemned to the second death, from which there is no recovery. The Syriac reading takes from the Universalist this, which is one of his chief proof texts. Christ is not the Savior of the world in the sense in which this word is usually taken by him — but He is a *Redeemer* of the world, as the Syriac shows, but the LIFE-GIVER of only those who believe on His name. "It is appointed unto men *once* to die, but after this the judgment." "For God so loved the world that He gave His only begotten Son, that *whosoever believeth* in Him should not perish but have Everlasting Life."

The Syriac Peshito canon of the New Testament closes here. Without going on to notice the few cases of this word that occur in the remaining books, as they were subsequently added, we may well conclude our review with the following summary remarks.

Our criticism lies, not against the Greek words *Sōzō*, *Sōtēr*, and *Sōtēria*, nor against their rendering in our version, because of what they express, but because of what they fail to express. These words — or rather this word, for they may be treated as substantially one — may have respect to a mere temporal or temporary rescue, a salvation from physical evil, or peril, or to our redemption or resurrection from our Adamic

death, which includes the whole human family, as in
the passage last cited (1 John 4: 14,) or, supposing
the doctrine of endless sin and misery to be true, it
may have respect to our salvation from this fearful
doom. But all this, in the popular mind, is a salvation only FROM, and not TO, any thing. The force of
the word seems to have expended itself, and to stop
just here — a salvation *from ?* And this is just where
our modern theology is deficient. Man is said to be
immortal without any Savior. He has incurred by his
sins the penalty of endless sin and misery. Now what
he is thought to need is, not the gift of an Eternal
Life, but to be rescued or delivered or saved from
this doom, that he may pass his eternal life in the
blessedness and joy of heaven. As for an endless life,
he has it now, in his own right. It has not been forfeited ; it cannot be. But he must be rescued or
saved from the fearful doom to which he is exposed.
This is the great salvation of the Gospel, and Christ,
who saves him, is his Savior.

But this is a very low and meager view of Christ
and His Gospel. It takes no account of the great
boon, the gift He brings us. "The gift of God is
Eternal LIFE through Jesus Christ our Lord." "I
give unto them Eternal LIFE," says Christ. This is
indeed constantly reiterated throughout the New Testament, in all our versions, but the Grecian philosophy, that dominates our theological schools, and
which has put its interpretation on our Greek and
English versions, has contrived to give such a spiritu-
alistic, ethical interpretation to this word "Life," and
to its opposite "Death," as to save the Platonic doctrine of the natural immortality of all men, and to
make these words "life" and "death" mean, simply
states of being; one a state of endless blessedness,
and the other a state of endless sin and misery, so
that these words *Save, Savior, Salvation,* simply in the
sense of rescue, exactly express all its advocates would
have them express, and only this.

But when we turn to the Syriac (Peshito) New
Testament, which certainly ante-dates as a collection

of the sacred writings every other collection; which
was made even during the lifetime of most of the
Apostles, and which is in the vernacular of the Jews
of that age, and which gives the very words of our
Lord and His immediate disciples, we find this great
Gospel truth brought out so fully, so clearly, so
emphatically, and so repeatedly, as to put it beyond
the possibility of cavil or dispute with those who
receive these Scriptures as the Word of God.

In the one hundred and twenty or more instances
cited in the foregoing paper, in which the Greek
word *Sōzō* occurs, either as a verb or noun, and generally translated *Save, Savior, Salvation,* in our version, we find that in every case, where the salvation
in question is evidently a temporal rescue or deliverance, a salvation *from ?* a word is used in the Syriac
to express this idea, such as *rescue, restore, cure, re-
deem,* or *save,* etc. But in all the other cases, where
the Gospel boon or gift is spoken of — including the
great majority of cases — the higher specific word signifying TO GIVE LIFE, *The gift of* LIFE, The LIFE-
GIVER, is employed. If this distinctive representation had been carried into the Greek, as it is not, and
into our version, where it is also wanting, it would
seem to have been absolutely impossible to have lost
this prime Gospel doctrine out of our Christian theology, or to have obscured it to the mind of the common reader.

And now, if all who believe in this central doctrine
of IMMORTALITY and ETERNAL LIFE only in Christ,
would go back to the primitive mode of expressing
the doctrine they hold, and use, instead of the words
Save, Salvation, Savior, which are but partial and
ambiguous at best, the more expressive and definite
words To LIVE, LIFE, our LIFE-GIVER, as the first disciples did, we might perhaps do something toward
restoring the primitive faith in this leading doctrine
of the Gospel : — ETERNAL LIFE AS THE GIFT OF GOD
THROUGH JESUS CHRIST OUR LIFE-GIVER.

PHILADELPHIA, PA., March, 1886.
3*

(*From the Rainbow, London, England.*)

LITERARY NOTICE,

By Rev. Edward White,

Pres. of the Congregational Union of England and Wales.

THE UNSPEAKABLE GIFT

OF ETERNAL LIFE THROUGH JESUS CHRIST OUR LORD.

By J. H. Pettingell, A.M.

Mr. Pettingell, whose name is familiar to our readers, is perhaps, now that Prof. Hudson, of Cambridge, Mass., is dead, the most accomplished and persistent advocate of the doctrine of LIFE in Christ, in the United States; and this book is the maturest labor of his pen. He has condensed into this admirable duodecimo, the substance of the whole controversy on immortality during the last thirty years, and exhibited the result in a style of singular clearness, force, and penetration. If we were asked to mention any work, which, while not too elaborate, was yet fitted to satisfy scholars, without being unintelligible to ordinary educated readers, we should certainly fix on this book of Mr. Pettingell's as deserving of this recommendation. The entrance of a single copy of this cheap and well printed volume into any congregation would inevitably commence a theological revolution of a wholesome description. . . . We most heartily commend this volume to our readers, begging them to observe that it is sold in England by Mr. Elliot Stock, of London.

Mr. Pettingell has conferred a service of inestimable value upon the English reading world by this, the crowning labor of his life. It is introduced to the American public by a brief preface from the pen of Mr. Edward White, of London.

Mr. Pettingell shows a wide acquaintance with the literature of the discussion, and his benignant temper is such as to obtain a hearing for his case from all except envenomed "disputers of this world." The "man of God" appears in every page dealing with divine truths in a divine manner.

The book is beautifully bound in fine muslin, with back and side title.   Published by

I. C. WELLCOME, Yarmouth, Me.

Price $1.00. Postage free

THE UNSPEAKABLE GIFT.

BY J. H. PETTINGELL, A.M.

COMMENDATORY NOTICES.

The first edition (of 1,000) of the Unspeakable Gift was exhausted within two months from the time of its first appearance. We subjoin a few of the many notices that have been received.

From REV. EDWARD WHITE, London, Eng.

"I think it the fullest, calmest, the ablest, and most Christian representation of conditional immortality hitherto made. Your work is most admirably done. The style is very pure and forcible. As for the chapter of contrasted parallels at the end, it is splendid. I wish it were republished in England."

From REV. GEO. R. KRAMER, Brooklyn, N. Y.

"That man is essentially immortal is neither the utterance of Reason or Revelation, but that those who are qualified for immortality will receive it is the suggestion of Reason and the promise of Revelation. All this is ably presented by Mr. Pettingell in this work. Mr. Pettingell's book is a scholarly work, and his style is forcible. This book is the work of an educated man, who, accepting the word of God as a little child, ' has been redeemed from the vain corruption received by tradition of his fathers.'"

From the CHRISTIAN AT WORK.

"Whether agreeing or disagreeing with the author's teaching that none but the righteous will gain immortality, and that all others must utterly perish, this recent book will be found intensely interesting."

From REV. W. LEASK, D.D., London, Eng. (in the "Rainbow").

"Mr. Pettingell has done well in the fidelity of his testimony to the central truth of Scriptures—Eternal Life only in Christ. He sees this as the sublime meaning of redemption, and he also sees the abounding theological confusion caused by blindness to this fact. This his last work, though not his least, is marked by a fulness of thought and clearness of expression which the intelligent reader will know how to appreciate."

From the HERALD AND PRESBYTER, Cincinnati, O.

"The doctrine of this work is that immortality is the gift of God through Jesus Christ, and is the portion only of believers; while the wicked, though raised at the judgment, will, after the judgment, be literally destroyed. The author appears to have examined the question with much care, in which he displays a large amount of literary and biblical scholarship. In all other respects he holds the general system of doctrine common to evangelical Christians. Whether his views are accepted or not, he will not fail to command the respect of the reader."

From the PHILADELPHIA METHODIST.

"The author distinctively shows that eternal life is the gift of God through Jesus Christ; that none but the righteous will gain immortality; that all others must utterly perish. The author shows conclusively that it was God's original purpose to give immortality to man, but having fallen by sin he can only be restored through

1

Christ. We want more of the power of this 'unspeakable gift' to overcome sin and secure holiness."

From the CHRISTIAN STANDARD, Pittsburg, Pa.

"Mr. Pettingell is a pleasant writer, and shows no mean ability in arranging his arguments in defence of his positions. Indeed, we know of no book in advocacy of the same views that makes a more plausible showing of that side of the question."

From THE INTERIOR, Chicago, Ill.

"This book is an earnest, courteous, and fairly creditable endeavor to prove that immortality does not come from Adam by natural birth, and is not, consequently, the natural endowment of every man, but that it is a supernatural endowment derived from Christ, and only by a new spiritual birth and a resurrection from the dead."

From the CENTRAL BAPTIST, St. Louis, Mo.

"The author is a man of extensive scholarship, and argues his points forcibly and earnestly, so that the book is a good defence of his views, whatever may be the opinions of the reader."

From the EDITOR OF RESTITUTION.

"No better book has yet been brought out than 'The Unspeakable Gift.' It is emphatically *the book for the times*."

From the ILLUSTRATED WEEKLY.

"Mr. Pettingell argues with great earnestness, evidently believing that he is upholding the cardinal truth of the gospel."

From the CHRISTIAN STATESMAN, Milwaukee, Wis.

"If we rightly understand this author, it is that immortality is not inherent in man, but is the gift of our Lord Jesus Christ. As a practical fact, nothing is plainer to us than that it is true. There is no immortality, eternal life, without Christ. It is a duty to read such books. This book contains a vast amount of authorities on the subject."

From the METHODIST RECORDER, Philadelphia, Pa.

"The author of this volume is a thoughtful, scholarly and reverent writer. His position is that eternal life is the gift of God through Jesus Christ. While those who believe in Christ shall become immortal, those who reject him, he holds, will lose this boon, and perish forever—cease to be. The author presents his view with considerable clearness and force."

From the ZION'S HERALD, Boston, Mass.

"The writer is one of the ablest defenders of the doctrine of conditional, as distinguished from natural, immortality. He believes this (the immortal life) to be purely the gift of Christ. An immense amount of literature bearing upon the theme is gathered in this volume. The conviction and earnestness of the author as to the truth he utters are apparent on every page."

From MR. JAMES SPENCE, Madras, India.

"I have read the book with great pleasure and profit. It is just the book for the times, a compendium of the scriptural doctrine of Life in Christ, on its broadest platform."

From the (METHODIST) CHRISTIAN ADVOCATE, Richmond, Va.

"Mr. Pettingell has written several books, but this is said to be his best. It is plainly and strongly written, and will do good in these times of new creeds and new dogmas."

THE GOSPEL OF LIFE

IN THE

SYRIAC NEW TESTAMENT.

THE SYRIAC, PESHITO, CONTRASTED WITH THE GREEK, WITH
RESPECT TO THE FOLLOWING WORDS, VIZ.:

(GREEK.)	(English Version of the Greek.)	(English Version of the Syriac.)
SŌZŌ.	**Save.**	To give **Life.**
SŌTĒRIA.	**Salvation.**	The gift of **Life.**
SŌTĒR.	**Savior.**	The **Life-Giver.**

By J. H. PETTINGELL, A. M.

*Author of the "Homiletical Index," "Theological Trilemma,"
"Platonism versus Christianity," "Bible Terminology,"
"The Life Everlasting," "The Unspeakable Gift," "Lan-
guage—Its Nature and Functions," "The Two Ways,"
"Will Satan Live Forever?" "Human Immor-
tality," "Life and Death in the New Testa-
ment," "The Fact and Nature of the
Resurrection of the Dead," etc., etc.*

"Christ spoke and discoursed in the Syriac language." *Francius.*
"The greater part of the New Testament was *originally* written—I
believe—in Syriac, and not merely translated, in the Apostolic age."
Pres. E. Stiles, of Yale College.
"It is natural to suppose, from its great antiquity, that it must deviate in
many cases from the Greek manuscripts, the oldest of which were written
above four hundred years later, and are mostly the productions of countries remote from Syria." *Michaelis.*

YARMOUTH, ME.:

SCRIPTURAL PUBLICATION SOCIETY.

ADDRESS, I. C. WELLCOME.

Price, 15 Cents, by mail.

THE PLAN OF REDEMPTION.

SIXTH THOUSAND.

" We think it decidedly the best volume ever put forth. It far surpasses all my anticipations. It will shed new light upon all."—*Glad Tidings.*

" I think no one can carefully read the book without being benefited."— *Dr. J. Bates, Congregationalist.*

" It has given me more light on the Bible than I obtained in fifty years' study and meetings."—*R. Lufkin, Congregationalist.*

" I never read any book with so much satisfaction."—*J. N. Wate. Meth.*

" We all like the book. I wish you to send me ten dollars' worth to distribute among our children and friends."—*E. W. Wate, Baptist.*

" It is the best work, in many respects, that I ever read. It is a remarkable book. I have read it through five times."—*S. M. Adams.*

" It is the choicest book on that subject I ever read."—*Elder P. W. Houp*

" ' The Plan of Redemption.' I think it the best work I ever read on the Scriptures."—*Elder Rufus Baker.*

" I have been examining the book, 'The Plan of Redemption,' for myself. I must say here, that it is the most comprehensive and instructive work that I ever examined on any theological subject whatever." — *Elder M. B. Patterson.*

" Your book contains sublime ideas and deep thoughts. There are parts of it I like very much."—*W. H. Shailer, D. D.*

" The Plan of Redemption is one of the most important books I have ever read. All christians should read it."—*Prof. F. A. Slater, Ark.*

" I have just finished reading your book. It is so good I shall help circulate it. Send me one hundred copies." A second order. " I have sold and given all. Send me 100 copies more."—*Wm. Watson, De Kalb, Ill.*

" I heartily thank you for that excellent book, ' The Plan of Redemption.' It is a perfect treasure. I am delighted with it. I could find use for ten copies if I had them. I have loaned it to a Baptist brother. He is much pleased with it."—*J. Spence, Mission Agent, Madras, E. India.*

" Your beautiful book has been of great benefit to me. It sets forth the Plan of Redemption so clearly. We are having it translated into Tamil hoping to get funds to publish it for the natives of India."—*Rev. C. Massillamani, Missionary, South India.*

" I have read ' Plan of Redemption.' I like it much; how refreshing to get hold of the truth, and feel and know that it is the truth. Your tenth chapter interested me most; I wish I had it in tract form to distribute."— *D. D. Chaffee, Wilbraham, Mass.*

" I am greatly pleased with your book, 'The Plan of Redemption.' I think it the best work I ever read on the Scriptures."—*Eld. R. Baker.*

" I am highly pleased with your work, 'The Plan of Redemption;' it seems so clear and expressive of Scripture sentiments. I want to get it into the hands of every one." —*C. Tuller, West Point, N. Y.*

" It is just the book for the times. It is a book long needed. But few people are conversant with the plan of redemption as revealed in the Bible. and the authors seem to be fully aware of this fact, and have made the subject so plain that the child can understand it. I think Christians should do all they can to circulate this very important book."—*O. W. Kinball.*

We have nearly one thousand testimonies similar to the above, nearly fifty from men who were converted from Universalism by reading it.

All who want to engage in selling such a work, to benefit their fellowmen, and earn good pay, may address I. C. WELLCOME, Yarmouth, Me., with postage stamp, for terms. Our terms are liberal and safe.

Sixth thousand,—neatly bound in muslin, $1.25. Sent post-paid by mail.

Address,   **I. C. WELLCOME,**
                              Yarmouth, Me.

THE ONE FOLD AND ONLY DOOR,

By A. C. PALMER.

THIS IS AN IMPORTANT BOOK FOR THESE TIMES.

WE GIVE A FEW OF MANY NOTICES.

THE ONE FOLD AND THE ONLY DOOR is a book that is easily understood, and whilst it attacks the error of the glorification of the saint at death, it presents in bold promontory conspicuousness the positive truth of a real, substantial, incorruptible recompense through Him who says, "I am the resurrection and the life." The argument is clear, very plain and strong. One is deeply impressed in reading this work of the absolute necessity of rising again in order to enter upon the grandeurs of the kingdom of God. Brooklyn, N. Y., *Rev. Geo. R. Kramer.*

It is one of the best books I ever read.—*E. Glidden.*

From Zions Herald.—THE ONE FOLD AND THE ONLY DOOR, by A. C. Palmer. This volume has much in it that a devout heart can enjoy. It teaches the actual unconsciousness of the dead until Christ's second coming, and then the resurrection to *eternal life* only of those who fall asleep in Him. The volume shows much ingenuity.

From The Portland Transcript.—From I. C. Wellcome we have a volume entitled THE ONE FOLD AND THE ONLY DOOR. It is a treatise in support of the dogma that the resurrection is a *future* event for all saints; that those who have died in the faith await the resurrection in an entirely unconscious state. The "better country" promised by God is not yet received by any of his saints. The Lord's people do not enter heaven one by one, but *en masse.* It shows that man's natural immortality is not taught in the Bible. The eternal death promised the wicked is literal. It will interest students of the Bible.

From The Congregationalist.—THE ONE FOLD AND THE ONLY DOOR, by A. C. Palmer, sets forth his idea of the Biblical teachings about our future life and abode. He has some peculiar ideas, such as that the soul actually does sleep from death until the resurrection, that all the redeemed then will enter heaven together, that the paradise promised by Jesus to the penitent thief is yet to be entered. Mr. Palmer writes with unfailing reverence and with the highest purpose. His views deserve the courteous heed of Biblical students.

From The Interior, Chicago.—In THE ONE FOLD AND THE ONLY DOOR A. C. Palmer endeavors to disprove the doctrine of natural immortality. He insists that conscious life ends at death to good and bad alike, that believers do not go immediately to heaven, but that they, too, remain in a state of death till Christ at his second coming gives them resurrection and life.

From The Central Baptist, St. Louis.—This book discusses in a calm and thoughtful way the doctrines of which it treats; meeting much of modern error and bringing forth much of truth.

From The Bath Times.—This is a well-written, critical, instructive, valuable, and timely book, in a remarkable kindly spirit and forcible arguments. Neatly bound in fine muslin, gilt back, and gilt side title.

From Messiah's Advocate, Cal.—It treats in a clear style ❡ the Necessity of the Resurrection, God, the God of the Living, Paul's Desire to Depart, The Thief on the Cross, our Earthly Home, Rich Man and Lazarus, Transfiguration, Spirits in Prison, and many other things, bringing out old truths in a neat volume.

From The World's Crisis, Boston.—This is a well made book, written by A. C. Palmer. The author discusses, with clearness and ability, "The Unseen Things, The Gathering; Resurrection; A Knotty Question Answered; The One Fold; Christ and the Penitent Thief; Paradise and the Third Heaven; The Rich Man and Lazarus," etc., etc. This work should have a liberal patronage.

Neatly bound, gilt back, and gilt side title. Price, 60 cents, by mail.

THE SCRIPTURAL PUBLICATION SOCIETY,

Yarmouth, Maine.   Address, I. C. WELLCOME.

AN OPEN LETTER

TO THE EDITOR OF THE "CONGREGATIONALIST,"

Being a Reply to an answer given in the "Congregationalist," to a correspondent who asked the editor's views as to the strength of the proof of Conditional Immortality.

BY REV. J. H. PETTINGELL, A. M.,

Author of the "Theological Trilemma," "Platonism vs. Christianity," "The Life Everlasting," "Bible Terminology," "The Unspeakable Gift," etc.

$2.00 per 100; 35 cents per dozen, by mail.

A REPLY TO REV. JOHN GREENE, A. M.,

——ON——

"LIFE AND DEATH IN THE NEW TESTAMENT."

In the Baptist Quarterly Review for December, 1884.

BY J. H. PETTINGELL, A.M.

$2.00 per 100; 35 cents per dozen, by mail.

A REPLY TO PROF. W. G. T. SHEDD, D.D., LL.D.,

——ON——

"THE CERTAINTY OF ENDLESS PUNISHMENT,"

In the North American Review for February, 1885.

BY J. H. PETTINGELL, A. M.

$2 00 per 100; 35 cents per dozen, by mail.

THE TWO WAYS,

THE WAY OF LIFE AND THE WAY OF DEATH.

An Address before the Young Ministers' Christian Union, at Providence, R. I., Aug. 6, 1885. Repeated before the Association for the Promotion of Christian Knowledge, at Brooklyn, N. Y., Sept. 27, 1885.

BY J. H. PETTINGELL, A. M.

$4.00 per 100; 50 cents per dozen, by mail.

THE FACT AND THE NATURE OF

THE RESURRECTION OF THE DEAD;

HISTORICAL, DOCTRINAL, SCRIPTURAL.

An Address before the General Convention of Ministers and Laymen, at Worcester, Mass , Nov. 11, 1885.

BY J. H. PETTINGELL, A. M.

$2.00 per 100; 35 cents per dozen, by mail.

THE GOSPEL OF ETERNAL LIFE.

A REPLY TO REV. J. H. BROOKES, D. D.,

ON ANNIHILATION.

In "THE TRUTH," FOR NOVEMBER AND DECEMBER, 1885.

BY J. H. PETTINGELL, A. M.

Price of each of the above works, 5 cents, by mail.

YARMOUTH, ME.:

SCRIPTURAL PUBLICATION SOCIETY.

Address   I. C. WELLCOME.

www.ingramcontent.com/pod-product-compliance
Lightning Source LLC
Chambersburg PA
CBHW021525090426
42739CB00007B/782